MEAL-PREP COOKBOOK

Easy and Delicious Meal Prep Recipes for Beginners

Edward Cruz

You must not rely on the information in the book as an alternative to medical advice from your doctor or other professional healthcare provider. If you have any specific questions about any medical matter you should consult your doctor or other professional healthcare provider. If you think you may be suffering from any medical condition you should seek immediate medical attention. You should never delay seeking medical advice, disregard medical advice, or discontinue medical treatment because of information in this book.

Free Bonus Book

"365 Keto Diet Recipes"

Get a link for the Bonus book at the end of this book

CONTENTS

Introduction   1

APPETIZERS   5

Baked Avocado Slices   6

Breaded Cauliflower with Parmesan Cheese   9

Creamy Oreo Cookies   12

Muffins with Quinoa, Spinach and Sun-dried Tomatoes   15

Saganaki - Fried Cheese   18

Salty Cake "Tourlou"   21

BREAKFAST   24

"Accelerator" Pomegranate Ginger Smoothie   25

Almond Peach Smoothie   28

Baked Apple Pancake   31

Blueberry and Honey Granola Bars   34

Cocoa Crepes with Stevia   37

Crescent Ground Beef and Parmesan   40

Delicious Sausage Breakfast Casserole   43

Grits Berries Mush   46

Maple Custard French toast   49

Power Blast Morning Smoothie   52

Rustic Cornbread with Cheese   55

Savory Corn Muffins with Leeks   58

Simple Bread with Spinach and Cheese 61

Summer Tropical Smoothie 64

MAIN DISH/MEAL 67

"Breaded" Tuna Patties 68

Baked Shrimp with Peppers and Sun-dried Tomatoes 71

Beef and Vegetables Stew 74

Braised Green Beans with Tomato and Parsley 77

Braised Pork with Eggplants and Peppers 80

Braised Squid and Potato Stew 83

Chicken and Peppers Risotto 86

Creamy Green Split Peas Chowder 89

Halibut and Celery Casserole 92

Japanese Style Mushroom Shrimp Stew 95

Lamb Fricassee with Lettuce 98

Lemony Artichokes with Fresh Dill 101

Marinated and Grilled Pork Cutlets 104

Pork Fillets with Mustard Mushrooms Sauce 107

WARM SALADS 110

Beetroot Leaves Salad with Broccoli and Sheep Cheese 111

Golden Vegetables with Balsamic Vinegar 114

Greek Salad - Horta, Asparagus and Cheese Sauce 117

Warm Salad with Artichokes, Peas and Sour Dressing 120

Warm Salad with Avocado 123

Warm Salad with Green Beans, Bacon & Potatoes 126

PIZZA 129

Angelo Bianco Pizza 130

Delicious Greek Pizza 133

Double Cheese Turkey Pizza 137

Easy Homemade Pizza 140

Four - Cheese and Rosemary Pizza 143

Italiana Cremini Funghi Pizza 146

Peach and Pineapple Pepperoni Pizza 149

Simple Margarita Pizza 152

SOUPS/STEWS 155

Avgolemono - Greek Traditional Chicken Soup 156

Chicken, Cabbage and Apple Stew 159

Creamy Basil Sun-Dried Tomato Soup 162

Creamy Zucchini and Potato Soup 165

Healthy Nettle Soup with Feta 168

Instant Broccoli Soup 171

Instant Chicken and Arugula Soup 174

Instant Sweet Potato Soup with Coconut Milk 177

Light Collard Greens Soup 180

Mediterranean Octopus Stew 183

Pesto Chicken and Spinach Soup 186

Smooth Cauliflower Soup 189

Tomato Soup with Rice 192

Winter Turkey Stew 195

FINGER FOOD/SNACKS 198

Baked Zucchini Patties 199

Delicious Butter Bannock 202

Instant Asparagus Sticks 205

Keto Parmesan Triangles 208

Raspberry Muffins (Gluten-free; Sugar-free) 211

Savory Sesame Sticks 214

Zucchini "Ducats" with Parmesan and Herbs 217

SAUCES/DRESSING — 220
  Delicious Parsley Dip — 221
  Skordalia - Crushed Garlic Sauce — 224
  Homemade Basil Sauce with Pine Nuts — 227
  Homemade Roquefort Sauce — 230
  Hot Tropical Sauce — 233
  Mushroom Sauce (for Roasted Meat) — 237
CASSEROLES — 240
  Absolute Summer Vegetable Casseroles — 241
  Artichoke Hearts with Peas and Potato Casserole — 244
  Bacon - Pork and Vegetables Casserole — 247
  Beef and Orzo Giouvetsi Casseroles — 250
  Mediterranean Feta and Vegetable Casserole — 253
  Pork with Mustard and Horseradish Casserole — 256
  Spicy Spanish Rice Casserole — 259
SWEETS/DESSERTS — 262
  Cognac - Chocolate Roll — 263
  Cranberries and Hazelnuts Muffins — 266
  Dark Knight Cake — 270
  Oat - Flake Cookies with Raisins — 273
  Total Chocolate Cake — 276
  Traditional Semolina Cake with Syrup — 279
VEGETARIAN — 282
  Braised Cauliflower with Grated Tomato (Crock Pot) — 283
  Braised Celeriac with Dill — 286
  Dalmatian Braised Swiss Chard Dish — 289
  Green Bean Power Soup (Slow Cooker) — 292
  Mediterranean Green Beans with Potato — 295

Vegetable and Almond Paradise Patties   298

PIES/PASTRIES   301

   Cheesy Mushrooms - Bacon Pie   302

   Pumpkin Pie with Feta   305

   Perfect Crustless Sausage, Mushrooms and Spinach Quiche   308

   Potato Pie with Soft Goat Cheese   311

   Traditional Cretan Tomato Pie   314

   Wild Greens Pie with Feta and Yoghurt   318

Bonus Book   322

About the Author   323

INTRODUCTION

Becoming a great cook is a journey full of exploration, browsing the isles in search of novel ingredients and tasting all the different aromas. There is a bit of applied chemistry and just a dash of alchemy in every tasty meal, as we turn plain ingredients into a wondrous mix of flavor, texture, and scent. But cooking is meant to be practical as well.

The idea of making our own meals just the way we like and having them frozen is the pinnacle of convenience. Especially when kids come a-knocking and start reaching for candy and snacks before going out on daily adventures, it's time to whip out a homemade meal to have them satiated and on a healthy diet. Since kids have very little patience it takes a miracle to distract them long enough to make a meal from scratch, so again it works best if a meal is made ahead and frozen. Knowing when the kids come back from school or play and heating up a meal at just the right moment is a magical parenting skill that's worth its weight in gold.

It's the Ninjas Cutting Onions

The best part about scaling meals up is doing less washing and cleaning that usually accompanies a homemade meal. Rather than chopping onions and tearing up seven times a week for seven meals and washing everything seven times over you can chop all of it in one go, clean everything and savor the tear-free time. What's interesting is how much time and mental energy we lose just switching from one task to another or simply to get in the zone and just do any given task efficiently; by preparing large batches of ingredients it's easy to avoid distractions that usually appear when we're constantly switching tasks.

When the humongous meal is cooked you can split it into disposable containers to be frozen in. This allows you to reheat and serve the portions while simply chucking the containers afterward, so it's even less juggling the dirty pots, pans, and plates. Getting that spotless shiny kitchen looks from shows and magazines isn't really possible unless you resort to tricks like this that come down to cooking spates and long cool down periods in between where you can really take your time with scrubs to make the kitchen absolutely impeccable. Once the pressure is off to constantly cook and clean, clean and cook you can really make both cooking and cleaning a relaxed, enjoyable experience that delivers.

The Best Way to Shore up Health

A frozen homemade meal is also a great backup for when there's an avalanche of domestic mishaps and distractions; you always have at least something to serve as a meal to stave the hunger off while dealing with the crisis. It bears repeating just how devastating an irregular diet can be to a young body, in particular when it comes to blood sugar. When we eat something our 30-foot digestive tract starts mauling the food using acid and digestive enzymes to extract energy and nutrients in a way our body can process them. It all starts seeping into the bloodstream for cells to draw as needed but if meals are continually skipped the level of energy in the blood, also known as blood sugar level, falls down drastically and the body pretty much goes haywire trying to lasso the hormones and bodily functions.

A Meal Made in a Lab

It's even worse if the homemade meal is then replaced by a glob of industrially processed food that usually gets loaded with salt, sugar, and fat to cover over defects in manufacturing and make it as appealing as possible, literally causing addiction and maybe even diabetes somewhere down the line. Cereals, potato chips, and candy are arguably the worst kinds of food that are still edible and represent subsistence food reserved for famished people who will otherwise starve. This artificial food cause rapid blood sugar swings that impact the liver the most, as it struggles to balance things out. Worse yet, this food is also loaded with "generally recognized as safe"additives to prolong its shelf life and make it crunchier, juicier, colorful or otherwise more marketable. One such ingredient that was consumed for decades before causing health issues was gluten, a wheat protein used as a thickener since the 1930s in ice creams to make them melt slower. Also "generally recognized as safe", gluten was gradually added in ever-increasing quantities to pretty much every product as a cheap bulker until people started having allergic reactions to it, leading to a backlash and total withdrawal from the market some 80 years later.

Fake Food that Tastes Like the Real Thing

High fructose corn syrup is an intensely sweet substitute for sugar that was meant to replace it due to being cheaper; the irony is that any ingredient the food industry sets its sights on soon becomes extremely expensive due to high demand, forcing a constant hunt for yet another "generally recognized as safe" replacement. High fructose corn syrup was also meant to actually reduce the number of sugars consumed but since marketability of a product, especially one aimed at kids, increases with sweetness the syrup started being used as a cheap bulker until it started repeating the exact same pattern we've seen with gluten.

Cocoa butter is next in line to be replaced with cheap chemicals that have the same taste and longer shelf life, in this case, polyglycerol polyricinoleate (PGPR). Under FDA regulations, consumables in the US cannot be marketed as "chocolate" unless they contain genuine cocoa butter that's painstakingly harvested from relatively few spots on the planet, so the industrial chocolate manufacturers introduced marketing terms "can't believe it's not chocolate" and "chocolatey" in products that contain PGPR to avoid false advertising lawsuits and just let the naiveté of the consumers do the rest.

Creating Our Own Eating Experience

The idea of meals made ahead of time is about being able to customize each batch to whoever's a need, such as making vegetarian, gluten-free or spicy food for each member of our household; if we happen to get unannounced guests we again have at least something to offer and put our best meal forward.

APPETIZERS

◆ ◆ ◆

Baked Avocado Slices

Ingredients

1 Tbsp fresh butter

2 avocado

1/2 cup breadcrumbs

1 egg beaten

1/4 cup Parmesan cheese

Instructions

1. Preheat oven to 360 F/180 C.
2. Grease a baking pan with the butter; set aside.
3. Cut the avocado into slices.
4. Beat the egg with a fork in a bowl.
5. Dip avocado slices in beaten egg mixture.
6. Roll the avocado slices trough bread crumbs.

7. In the end, roll avocado slices in the parmesan cheese.
8. Place breaded avocado slices into the prepared baked pan.
9. Bake for 15 minutes.
10. Remove from the oven and allow cooling.
11. Wrap in a kitchen paper, and place in plastic bag.
12. Keep refrigerated up to 5 days.

Servings: 3

Preparation Time: 25 minutes

Nutrition Facts

Serving size: 1/3 of a recipe (6 ounces)

Percent daily values based on the Reference Daily Intake (RDI) for a 2000 calorie diet.

Nutrition information calculated from recipe ingredients.

Amount per Serving

Calories 357,39

Calories From Fat (63%) 226,41

% Daily Value

Total Fat 26,54g 41%

Saturated Fat 7,06g 35%

Cholesterol 79,51mg 27%

Sodium 292,59mg 12%

Potassium 654,57mg 19%

Total Carbohydrates 23,38g 8%

Fiber 8,65g 35%

Sugar 1,6g

Protein 10g 20%

Breaded Cauliflower with Parmesan Cheese

Ingredients

1 cauliflower head cut into small florets

2 eggs

1 cup of flour

1 cup of breadcrumbs

1 cup parmesan grated

Olive oil for frying

Instructions

1. Boil the cauliflower floret in a large saucepan with salted water for about around 10 minutes.
2. Remove from water, drain in a colander and rinse with cold water.
3. Whisk the eggs in a small ball.
4. Combine the flour, Parmesan and the bread crumbs in a separate bowl.
5. Heat the oil in a large frying skillet.
6. Dip cauliflower in a flour/Parmesan mixture, and then dip in a whisked eggs.
7. Fry the cauliflower floweret 3 - 5 minutes or until getting a golden color.
8. Drain on a kitchen paper, and allow it to cool to room temperature.
9. Store in a plastic container with the lid, and refrigerate for 4 to 5 days.

Servings: 6

Preparation Time: 25 minutes

Nutrition Facts

Serving size: 1/6 of a recipe (6.9 ounces)

Percent daily values based on the Reference Daily Intake (RDI) for a 2000 calorie diet.

Nutrition information calculated from recipe ingredients.

Amount per Serving

Calories 386,44

Calories from Fat (49%) 187,91

% Daily Value

Total Fat 21,29g 33%

Saturated Fat 5,58g 28%

Cholesterol 76,67mg 26%

Sodium 440,35mg 18%

Potassium 394,56mg 11%

Total Carbohydrates 34,52g 12%

Fiber 3,33g 13%

Sugar 3,26g

Protein 14,94g 30%

Creamy Oreo Cookies

Ingredients

1 cup of cheese cream cheese

1 cup of butter

1 cup of sugar

1 cup of flour

1 pinch of salt

10 cookies crumbled in small pieces

Instructions

1. Heat oven to 350°F/175 C.
2. Mix the cheese with the butter and the sugar.
3. Beat with an electric mixer until all sugar is dissolved.
4. Slowly add the flour and a pinch of salt.

5. Continue to beat until all ingredients are combined well.
6. Add crumbled Oreo cookies and stir well.
7. Pour the dough in a baking pan and bake for 15 - 18 minutes.
8. Remove cookies from the oven and allow them to cool.
9. Keep refrigerated in a plastic bag or store in a freezer-safe bag, and keep in a freezer.

Servings: 12

Preparation Time: 30 minutes

Nutrition Facts

Serving size: 1/12 of a recipe (2.7 ounces)

Percent daily values based on the Reference Daily Intake (RDI) for a 2000 calorie diet.

Nutrition information calculated from recipe ingredients.

Amount per Serving

Calories 328,84

Calories from Fat (61%) 199,12

% Daily Value

Total Fat 22,65g 35%

Saturated Fat 13,55g 68%

Cholesterol 61,94mg 21%

Sodium 116,56mg 5%

Potassium 50,58mg 1%

Total Carbohydrates 29,89g 10%

Fiber 0,44g 2%

Sugar 19,11g

Protein 2,79g 6%

Muffins with Quinoa, Spinach and Sun-dried Tomatoes

Ingredients

1 1/4 cups frozen spinach

1 1/4 cups self-rising flour

3 free-range eggs

1/2 cup milk

1/4 cup fresh butter

1/2 cup of quinoa, cooked

5 oz sun-dried tomatoes

5 ounces Gouda cheese finely grated

Olive oil

Salt and ground black pepper

Instructions

1. Preheat your oven to 360 F/180 C.
2. Heat the butter in a non-stick pan and sauté the spinach on medium heat 3-5 minutes.
3. Sprinkle with the salt; stir and put it in a bowl.
4. Whisk the eggs with milk in a separate bowl.
5. Slowly add the flour and some melted butter; stir well.
6. Add the sun-dried tomatoes, boiled quinoa, spinach, grated hard cheese, and salt and pepper.
7. Stir until the ingredients are combined well.
8. Grease the muffins tin with olive oil, and distribute a mixture evenly into each muffins hole.
9. Bake in the oven for 20-25 minutes.
10. When the muffins are ready, allow cooling on room temperature.
11. Place in a plastic or glass container and keep refrigerated up to one week.

Servings: 12

Preparation Time: 35 minutes

Nutrition Facts

Serving size: 1/12 of a recipe (4.2 ounces)

Percent daily values based on the Reference Daily Intake (RDI) for a 2000 calorie diet.

Nutrition information calculated from recipe ingredients.

Amount per Serving

Calories 258,17

Calories From Fat (53%) 137,71

% Daily Value

Total Fat 15,71g 24%

Saturated Fat 7,21g 36%

Cholesterol 83,03mg 28%

Sodium 428,67mg 18%

Potassium 370,13mg 11%

Total Carbohydrates 21,1g 7%

Fiber 2,45g 10%

Sugar 1,24g

Protein 9,33g 19%

Saganaki - Fried Cheese

Ingredients

5 oz cheese (Gruyere or Pecorino Romano cheese)

2 Tbsp of flour

Olive oil for frying

1 lemon

Instructions

1. Cut cheese in rectangular pieces.
2. Dip cheese in cold water and then dip it in the flour, and shake it to remove the excess flour.
3. This will help the saganaki to keep its shape when fried and form a nice crisp crust.
4. Heat the oil in a frying pan and fry the saganaki until

golden on both sides.
5. Store in a plastic or glass container and keep refrigerated up to 3 - 4 days.
6. Serve with lemon juice and lemon slices.

Servings: 4

Preparation Time: 20 minutes

Nutrition Facts

Serving size: 1/4 of a recipe (6 ounces)

Percent daily values based on the Reference Daily Intake (RDI) for a 2000 calorie diet.

Nutrition information calculated from recipe ingredients.

Amount per Serving

Calories 258,29

Calories From Fat (93%) 239,29

% Daily Value

Total Fat 27,12g 42%

Saturated Fat 3,74g 19%

Cholesterol 0mg 0%

Sodium 1,43mg < 1%

Potassium 43,6mg 1%

Total Carbohydrates 5,87g 2%

Fiber 1,37g 5%

Sugar 0,01g

Protein 0,73g 1%

Salty Cake "Tourlou"

Ingredients

3/4 cup flour

1/2 cup of milk

100 g Gruyere cheese grated

1 tomato

1 onion

1/2 eggplant

1 small zucchini, peeled

3/4 cup of olive oil

Few fresh mint or basil leaves

1/2 cup parsley finely chopped

1 Tbsp of powdered yeast

Salt and freshly ground pepper to taste

Instructions

1. Preheat the oven to 360° F/ 180 °C.
2. Rinse, peel and cut all vegetables.
3. Heat 1/4 cup of olive oil in a frying skillet; sauté the onion with the pinch of salt for 3 minutes.
4. Add all vegetables and sauté over medium heat for 2 - 3 minutes; season with the salt and pepper and stir.
5. Allow it to cool in a colander and place in a large bowl.
6. Add the flour in a deep bowl along with yeast; knead for 2 - 3 minutes.
7. Add the olive oil and warm milk.
8. Continue to stir until getting a compact mixture.
9. Add vegetables, the salt and pepper, and fresh mint or basil leaves, and stir until all ingredients are combined well.
10. Place the dough in an oiled baking dish and bake for 45 minutes.
11. Remove from the oven and allow it to cool at room temperature.
12. Cut in slices, place in aluminum paper and place in a plastic bag.
13. Store in refrigerator for 4 - 5 days or store in a freezer-safe container, and keep in a freezer.

Servings: 8

Preparation Time: 1 hour and 5 minutes

Nutrition Facts

Serving size: 1/8 of a recipe (5.6 ounces)

Percent daily values based on the Reference Daily Intake (RDI) for a 2000 calorie diet.

Nutrition information calculated from recipe ingredients.

Amount per Serving

Calories 307,83

Calories From Fat (72%) 221,01

% Daily Value

Total Fat 25,04g 39%

Saturated Fat 5,43g 27%

Cholesterol 14,97mg 5%

Sodium 93,22mg 4%

Total Carbohydrates 15,15g 5%

Fiber 2,57g 10%

Sugar 3,29g

Protein 7,09g 14%

BREAKFAST

◆ ◆ ◆

"Accelerator" Pomegranate Ginger Smoothie

Ingredients

1 frozen banana, cut into chunks

1 tsp freshly grated ginger

1 1/2 tsp peanut butter

1 cup Greek yogurt (plain and unsweetened)

1 cup pomegranate juice

A handful of fresh spinach leaves

Instructions

1. Place all ingredients in your fast speed blender and blend until smooth and creamy.
2. Pour the "Accelerator" Pomegranate Ginger Smoothie into freezer-safe Mason jars, and freeze.

Servings: 2

Preparation Time: 5 minutes

Nutrition Facts

Serving size: 1/2 of a recipe (7.5 ounces)

Percent daily values based on the Reference Daily Intake (RDI) for a 2000 calorie diet.

Nutrition information calculated from recipe ingredients.

Amount per Serving

Calories 152,64

Calories From Fat (24%) 36,96

% Daily Value

Total Fat 4,23g 7%

Saturated Fat 2,55g 13%

Cholesterol 11,31mg 4%

Sodium 50,85mg 2%

Potassium 514,88mg 15%

Total Carbohydrates 26,42g 9%

Fiber 1,81g 7%

Sugar 19,42g

Protein 4,14g 8%

Almond Peach Smoothie

Ingredients

1 small peeled banana cut into 1-inch chunks and frozen

1 cup fresh baby spinach

1 cup orange juice

1 cup frozen peaches

3 Tbsp slivered almonds, toasted

Instructions

1. Dump all ingredients from the list above in a high-speed blender.
2. Blend until smooth and creamy.

3. Pour the smoothie into freezer-safe jars, and freeze.
4. Defrost and enjoy!

Servings: 2

Preparation Time: 10 minutes

Nutrition Facts

Serving size: 1/2 of a recipe (11.8 ounces)

Percent daily values based on the Reference Daily Intake (RDI) for a 2000 calorie diet.

Nutrition information calculated from recipe ingredients.

Amount per Serving

Calories 303,79

Calories From Fat (20%) 61,85

% Daily Value

Total Fat 7,39g 11%

Saturated Fat 0,64g 3%

Cholesterol 0mg 0%

Sodium 21,54mg < 1%

Potassium 787,69mg 23%

Total Carbohydrates 59,01g 20%

Edward Cruz

Fiber 5,7g 23%

Sugar 45,72g

Protein 5,42g 11%

Baked Apple Pancake

Ingredients

2 red apples, peeled, cored, thinly sliced

1/2 cup packed brown sugar

1/2 cup granulated sugar

2 tsp cinnamon

1 cup of milk

4 free-range eggs

1 cup all-purpose flour

Pinch of salt

1/4 cup fresh unsalted butter

Instructions

1. Preheat oven to 425 degrees F/260 C.
2. Oil 9x13-inch baking pan; set aside.
3. Toss apples with brown and granulated sugars, and cinnamon in a large bowl.
4. Whisk the milk, eggs, salt, and flour to combine well; you can use an electric mixer.
5. Dip apples in a flour mixture and place in a prepared baking pan.
6. Melt the butter and pour over the apples.
7. Bake for 20 to 30 minutes.
8. Allow cooling on room temperature.
9. Place in a container and cover with plastic freezer wrap. Keep in the freezer for two months.

Servings: 4

Preparation Time: 40 minutes

Nutrition Facts

Serving size: 1/4 of a recipe (9.5 ounces)

Percent daily values based on the Reference Daily Intake (RDI) for a 2000 calorie diet.

Nutrition information calculated from recipe ingredients.

Amount per Serving

Calories 544,08

Calories From Fat (28%) 153,09

% Daily Value

Total Fat 17,31g 27%

Saturated Fat 9,5g 48%

Cholesterol 199,06mg 66%

Sodium 174,09mg 7%

Potassium 283,26mg 8%

Total Carbohydrates 88,28g 29%

Fiber 2,37g 9%

Sugar 61,46g

Protein 11,15g 22%

Blueberry and Honey Granola Bars

Ingredients

1 1/2 cups of oats

1/4 cup brown sugar

3 Tbsp avocado oil

1/2 cup honey

2 tsp ground cinnamon

2 cups fresh blueberries

Instructions

1. Preheat oven to 350 F/170 C.
2. Grease with oil a 9 x 9-inch baking pan; set aside.
3. Place all ingredients in a saucepan and bring to boil; do not stir.
4. Pour the mixture in a prepared baking pan.
5. Place in oven and bake for about 40 minutes.
6. Allow it to cool completely and place in a fridge for 4 hours.
7. Remove from the fridge and cut into bars.
8. Store in a container, cover and keep refrigerated for one week or store in a freeze-safe bag, and keep in a freezer.

Servings: 8

Preparation Time: 50 minutes

Inactive Time: 4 hours

Nutrition Facts

Serving size: 1/8 of a recipe (3 ounces)

Percent daily values based on the Reference Daily Intake (RDI) for a 2000 calorie diet.

Nutrition information calculated from recipe ingredients.

Amount Per Serving

Calories 216,77

Calories From Fat (26%) 55,76

% Daily Value

Total Fat 6,37g 10%

Saturated Fat 0,79g 4%

Cholesterol 0mg 0%

Sodium 4,11mg < 1%

Potassium 105,85mg 3%

Total Carbohydrates 40,26g 13%

Fiber 2,79g 11%

Sugar 27,84g

Protein 2,36g 5%

Cocoa Crepes with Stevia

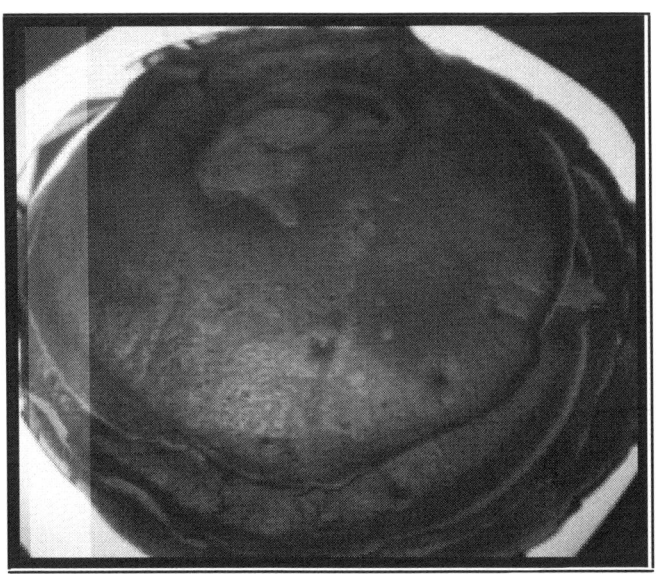

Ingredients

1 Tbsp fresh butter melted

2 Free-range eggs (beaten)

1 cup coconut milk (canned)

1/2 cup flour

2 Tbsp cocoa powder

1/4 cup stevia sweetener granulated

1 tsp vanilla powder (or extract)

Vegetable oil for frying

Instructions

1. Place all ingredients in your high-speed blender.
2. Blend until getting a compact mixture.
3. Heat the oil on a large frying pan over medium-high heat.
4. Pour the batter onto hot oil using approximately 1/4 cup for each crepe.
5. Cook each crepe for about 2 minutes.
6. Allow crepes to cool completely.
7. Place crepes between layers of parchment paper, and then place in freeze-safe plastic bags.
8. Keep refrigerated for 3 days or in a freezer for two months.

Servings: 6

Preparation Time: 20 minutes

Nutrition Facts

Serving size: 1/6 of a recipe (2.6 ounces)

Percent daily values based on the Reference Daily Intake (RDI) for a 2000 calorie diet.

Nutrition information calculated from recipe ingredients.

Amount per Serving

Calories 202,24

Calories From Fat (73%) 146,8

% Daily Value

Total Fat 16,95g 26%

Saturated Fat 6,38g 32%

Cholesterol 67,09mg 22%

Sodium 27,02mg 1%

Potassium 104,62mg 3%

Total Carbohydrates 10,15g 3%

Fiber 0,88g 4%

Sugar 0,21g

Protein 3,92g 8%

Crescent Ground Beef and Parmesan

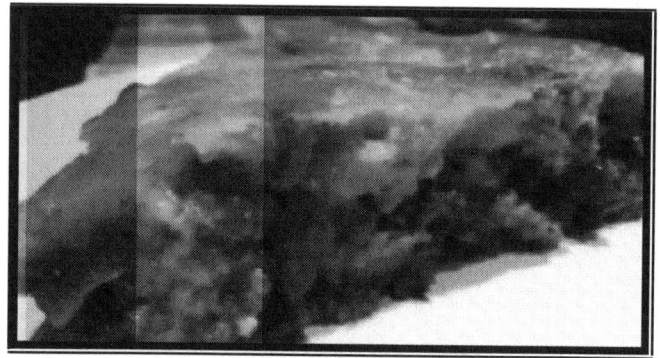

Ingredients

1 package crescent rolls

1 1/2 cups ground meat, cooked

1/2 cup Parmesan cheese freshly shredded

1 cup shredded hash brown potatoes

5 eggs

1-1/2 cups milk

1/4 cup fresh herbs to taste

Instructions

1. Preheat oven to 375 F/180C.
2. Line a baking pan with crescent dough.
3. Layer pastry with sausage, cheese, and potatoes.
4. Beat the eggs and milk. Pour over potatoes.

5. Sprinkle with Parmesan cheese and herbs.
6. Layer dough with ground beef, cheese, and hash brown potatoes.
7. Whisk the eggs with milk, a pinch of salt and fresh herb mixture; pour in baking pan
8. Bake for 30 to 40 minutes, or until golden brown.
9. Allow to cool, store in freezer-safe container and freeze.

Servings: 8

Preparation Time: 50 minutes

Nutrition Facts

Serving size: 1/8 of a recipe (6.9 ounces)

Percent daily values based on the Reference Daily Intake (RDI) for a 2000 calorie diet.

Nutrition information calculated from recipe ingredients.

Amount per Serving

Calories 385,88

Calories From Fat (47%) 182,13

% Daily Value

Total Fat 20,32g 31%

Saturated Fat 8,56g 43%

Cholesterol 155,82mg 52%

Sodium 1153,23mg 48%

Potassium 318,8mg 9%

Total Carbohydrates 32,95g 11%

Fiber 1,09g 4%

Sugar 6,44g

Protein 17,28g 35%

Delicious Sausage Break- fast Casserole

Ingredients

16 oz breakfast sausage, crumbled

4 cups bread cubes (preferably 2 - 3 days old)

2 cups grated Cheddar cheese

2 cups evaporated milk 1 light

10 free-range eggs, beaten

1 tsp dry mustard

1/4 tsp onion powder

Salt and ground black pepper to taste

Instructions

1. Preheat oven to 325° F/160 C.
2. Grease a 13 x 9-inch rectangular baking pan.
3. Place bread in a baking dish and generously sprinkle with cheese.
4. Whisk eggs with evaporated milk, dry mustard, onion powder and pinch salt and pepper in a bowl.
5. Pour the egg mixture evenly over bread and cheese.
6. Finally, sprinkle with crumbled sausages.
7. Bake for 60 to 65 minutes or until cheese is golden brown.
8. Allow cooling completely on room temperature.
9. Wrap in foil and pack in airtight container and place in a freezer.

Servings: 8

Preparation Time: 1 hour and 10 minutes

Nutrition Facts

Serving size: 1/8 of a recipe (7.9 ounces)

Percent daily values based on the Reference Daily Intake (RDI) for a 2000 calorie diet.

Nutrition information calculated from recipe ingredients.

Amount per Serving

Calories 542,69

Calories From Fat (64%) 348,03

% Daily Value

Total Fat 38,99g 60%

Saturated Fat 17,64g 88%

Cholesterol 323,94mg 108%

Sodium 881,12mg 37%

Potassium 430,59mg 12%

Total Carbohydrates 17,54g 6%

Fiber 0,59g 2%

Sugar 6,12g

Protein 29,13g 58%

Grits Berries Mush

Ingredients

1 1/2 cups milk

1 1/2 cups water

3/4 cup cooking grits

1/2 tsp salt

3 Tbsp honey strained

2 cups fresh or frozen blueberries, raspberries, red currants

Instructions

1. Heat the water and milk in a saucepan; bring to boil.
2. Slowly, add grits and the salt; give a good stir until well combined.

3. Reduce heat to a low, cover lid and cook about 8 to 10 minutes or until thickened completely.
4. Stir in honey and fruits; gently stir until all ingredients combined completely.
5. Store in a freezer-safe container and place in your freezer.

Servings: 4

Preparation Time: 20 minutes

Nutrition Facts

Serving size: 1/4 of a recipe (10.5 ounces)

Percent daily values based on the Reference Daily Intake (RDI) for a 2000 calorie diet.

Nutrition information calculated from recipe ingredients.

Amount per Serving

Calories 234,59

Calories From Fat (9%) 21,23

% Daily Value

Total Fat 2,41g 4%

Saturated Fat 1,22g 6%

Cholesterol 7,32mg 2%

Sodium 339,17mg 14%

Potassium 256,75mg 7%

Total Carbohydrates 48,24g 16%

Fiber 2,21g 9%

Sugar 21,1g

Protein 6,14g 12%

Maple Custard French toast

Ingredients

6 free-range eggs

1 cup milk

2 Tbsp maple syrup or honey

1-1/2 tsp cinnamon

Pinch of salt

12 slices of bread

2 Tbsp of fresh butter at room temperature

Instructions

1. Whisk together eggs, milk, maple syrup, cinnamon and salt in a bowl.
2. Dip bread slices in the egg mixture.
3. Heat the oil or butter in a large skillet over high heat.
4. Fry soaked bread slices for 1 minute (turning once).
5. Place a sheet of wax paper between each slice of bread, and then wrap in a heavy-duty freezer bag. Keep it in a freezer.

Servings: 6

Preparation Time: 15 minutes

Nutrition Facts

Serving size: 1/6 of a recipe (5.4 ounces)

Percent daily values based on the Reference Daily Intake (RDI) for a 2000 calorie diet.

Nutrition information calculated from recipe ingredients.

Amount per Serving

Calories 342,21

Calories From Fat (31%) 107,21

% Daily Value

Total Fat 12,06g 19%

Saturated Fat 5,11g 26%

Cholesterol 199,43mg 66%

Sodium 505,95mg 21%

Potassium 242,01mg 7%

Total Carbohydrates 43,3g 14%

Fiber 2,6g 10%

Sugar 9,39g

Protein 14,37g 29%

Power Blast Morning Smoothie

Ingredients

1 cup grape juice

1 frozen banana, cut into chunks

1 cup evaporated milk

1/2 cup kale (stems removed and coarsely chopped)

2 egg yolks

2 oz lemon juice

Instructions

1. Place all ingredients in your fast speed blender.
2. Blend 30 - 40 seconds or until smooth and creamy.
3. Pour the smoothie into the freezer-safe jar, and freeze.

Servings: 2

Total Time: 10 minutes

Nutrition Facts

Serving size: 1/2 of a recipe (9.8 ounces)

Percent daily values based on the Reference Daily Intake (RDI) for a 2000 calorie diet.

Nutrition information calculated from recipe ingredients.

Amount per Serving

Calories 226,93

Calories From Fat (20%) 45,33

% Daily Value

Total Fat 5,05g 8%

Saturated Fat 1,83g 9%

Cholesterol 185,23mg 62%

Sodium 163,53mg 7%

Potassium 781,31mg 22%

Total Carbohydrates 33,81g 11%

Fiber 1,97g 8%

Edward Cruz

Sugar 24,11g

Protein 13,67g 27%

Rustic Cornbread with Cheese

Ingredients

1 Tbsp olive oil

0.8 lb coarse ground corn flour

1 cup of water

1/2 sachet of baking powder

1 tsp of salt

1/2 cup of crumbled white cheese

Instructions

1. Preheat your oven to 420 F/ 210 C.
2. Grease a baking dish with olive oil; set aside.
3. Place the cornflour in a large bowl, and add water with

dissolved baking powder and salt.
4. Stir until all ingredients combined well.
5. Add the crumbled cheese and stir to combine well.
6. Place the cornflour mixture in a prepared baking dish.
7. Place in oven and bake for 15 - 20 minutes.
8. Remove from the oven and allow it to cool before slicing.
9. Wrap the slices in freezer paper and store in a freezer for one month.

Servings: 4

Preparation Time: 30 minutes

Nutrition Facts

Serving size: 1/4 of a recipe (3.7 ounces)

Percent daily values based on the Reference Daily Intake (RDI) for a 2000 calorie diet.

Nutrition information calculated from recipe ingredients.

Amount per Serving

Calories 126,22

Calories From Fat (34%) 43,05

% Daily Value

Total Fat 4,88g 8%

Saturated Fat 0,84g 4%

Cholesterol 0,62mg <1%

Sodium 666,14mg 28%

Potassium 193,9mg 6%

Total Carbohydrates 19,06g 6%

Fiber 1,6g 6%

Sugar 0,25g

Protein 2,37g 5%

Savory Corn Muffins with Leeks

Ingredients

1 lb of corn flour

1 cup of leek, finely chopped

1 1/2 cup of sparkling water

3/4 cup of olive oil

1 tsp baking powder, double acting

Salt to taste

Instructions

1. Preheat your oven to 400 F/220 C.
2. Grease with the olive oil a muffin tins; set aside.
3. Heat the oil in a frying pan and sauté a chopped leek with

salt for 5 - 6 minutes.

4. Remove the leek from the heat and allow to cool.
5. In a meantime, combine cornflour with the sparkling water, olive oil, baking powder, and salt; stir to combine well.
6. Add the leek and stir again to get a compact mixture.
7. Pour the mixture in a prepared muffin tin.
8. Bake for 20 minutes.
9. Allow to cool and wrap in a parchment paper and place in plastic bags; keep in a freeze for two months.

Servings: 6

Preparation Time: 35 minutes

Nutrition Facts

Serving size: 1/6 of a recipe (4.6 ounces)

Percent daily values based on the Reference Daily Intake (RDI) for a 2000 calorie diet.

Nutrition information calculated from recipe ingredients.

Amount per Serving

Calories 317,48

Calories From Fat (77%) 245,19

% Daily Value

Total Fat 27,78g 43%

Saturated Fat 3,84g 19%

Cholesterol 0mg 0%

Sodium 135,95mg 6%

Potassium 77,7mg 2%

Total Carbohydrates 16,81g 6%

Fiber 1,48g 6%

Sugar 0,58g

Protein 1,99g 4%

Simple Bread with Spinach and Cheese

Ingredients

3 eggs

1 cup of garlic-infused olive oil

2 cups of milk

2 cups of white flour

2 Tbsp of corn flour

1 baking powder

1 tsp of salt

1 cup of fresh spinach, chopped

1/2 cup goat cheese

Instructions

1. Preheat oven to 400 F/200 C.
2. Grease with the oil a rectangular baking pan.
3. Beat the eggs in a bowl.
4. Add the oil, milk corn and white flour, baking powder and the salt.
5. Stir with the fork until combined well.
6. Add the spinach and crumbled cheese; stir well.
7. Pour the mixture in a prepared baking pan.
8. Place in oven and bake for 20 - 25 minutes.
9. Allow to cool: cut in cubes.
10. Wrap the bread slices in a parchment paper and place in plastic bag. Keep in a freezer for one month.

Servings: 10

Preparation Time: 35 minutes

Nutrition Facts

Serving size: 1/10 of a recipe (5.3 ounces)

Percent daily values based on the Reference Daily Intake (RDI) for a 2000 calorie diet.

Nutrition information calculated from recipe ingredients.

Amount per Serving

Calories 357,18

Calories From Fat (64%) 228,33

% Daily Value

Total Fat 25,83g 40%

Saturated Fat 5,1g 26%

Cholesterol 56,96mg 19%

Sodium 393,67mg 16%

Potassium 200,72mg 6%

Total Carbohydrates 23,96g 8%

Fiber 1,69g 7%

Sugar 2,84g

Protein 8,06g 16%

Summer Tropical Smoothie

Ingredients

1 frozen banana, broken into pieces

1/2 cup pineapple, chopped into cubes

1/2 cup mango, peeled and chopped

1 cup spinach, fresh

2 cups coconut milk (canned)

2 carrots include leafy tops

1/2 cup coconut shredded, unsweetened

Instructions

1. Rinse and clean the carrots and all fruits.
2. Place carrots along with all remaining ingredients from the list in your high-speed blender.
3. Blend until smooth and creamy.
4. Pour the smoothie into Mason jars, and freeze for weeks in your freezer.

Servings: 4

Preparation Time: 5 minutes

Nutrition Facts

Serving size: 1/4 of a recipe (9 ounces)

Percent daily values based on the Reference Daily Intake (RDI) for a 2000 calorie diet.

Nutrition information calculated from recipe ingredients.

Amount per Serving

Calories 325,26

Calories From Fat (71%) 232,54

% Daily Value

Total Fat 27,78g 43%

Saturated Fat 24,42g 122%

Cholesterol 0mg 0%

Sodium 51,22mg 2%

Potassium 618,19mg 18%

Total Carbohydrates 21,38g 7%

Fiber 3,58g 14%

Sugar 11,03g

Protein 3,81g 8%

MAIN DISH/MEAL

◆ ◆ ◆

"Breaded" Tuna Patties

Ingredients

2 can (15 oz) tuna in oil, drained

1 cup bread crumbs

1 tsp of fresh thyme, chopped

3 Free-range eggs (beaten)

1 Lemon zest

1 cup Olive oil for frying

Instructions

1. Drain the tuna well and mix it with your fork.
2. Place all ingredients in a big shallow bowl, and stir well.
3. With your hands shape small patties.

4. Heat the oil in a frying pan over medium heat
5. Roll tuna patties first in bread crumbs, and then in beaten eggs.
6. Cook the tuna patties 3 - 4 minutes per side or until getting a nice golden brown color.
7. Allow cooling on room temperature.
8. Store in freezer-safe bags, and keep in a freezer.

Servings: 4

Preparation Time: 20 minutes

Nutrition Facts

Serving size: 1/4 of a recipe (10.8 ounces)

Percent daily values based on the Reference Daily Intake (RDI) for a 2000 calorie diet.

Nutrition information calculated from recipe ingredients.

Amount per Serving

Calories 589,14

Calories From Fat (51%) 340,61

% Daily Value

Total Fat 38,33g 59%

Saturated Fat 6,91g 35%

Cholesterol 228,75mg 76%

Sodium 1052,74mg 44%

Potassium 612,39mg 17%

Total Carbohydrates 20,06g 7%

Fiber 1,44g 6%

Sugar 1,88g

Protein 58,55g 117%

Baked Shrimp with Peppers and Sun-dried Tomatoes

Ingredients

15 large shrimps, cleaned, fresh or frozen

1 lemon juice

6 long green peppers

1 onion sliced

3 sun-dried tomatoes, preserved in oil

1 cup fresh tomato juice

1 tsp red chili pepper or to taste

2/3 cup olive oil

Salt and ground pepper to taste

Instructions

1. Put the shrimps in a bowl, squeeze half a lemon, and add a pinch of salt; stir.
2. Cover with a plastic cover and refrigerate for one hour to marinate.
3. Wash and remove the stalk and seeds from the peppers and place them in the baking pan.
4. Cut the rest of the herbs and melt the tomatoes.
5. Heat half the oil in a deep frying pan and sauté the onion and chili pepper until soft.
6. Then, add the tomatoes and tomato juice and let boil for 5 minutes; stir.
7. Preheat oven to 360F.
8. Remove the shrimp from the refrigerator and place in baking dish over the peppers.
9. Pour the sauce over the shrimps and add salt, freshly ground pepper and pour remaining oil.
10. Bake in the oven for 30-40 minutes or until golden brown.
11. Allow cooling on room temperature.
12. Store in the freeze-safer bag, and keep in a freezer.

Servings: 5

Preparation Time: 55 minutes

Inactive Time: 1 hour

Nutrition Facts

Serving size: 1/5 of a recipe (10.5 ounces)

Percent daily values based on the Reference Daily Intake (RDI) for a 2000 calorie diet.

Nutrition information calculated from recipe ingredients.

Amount per Serving

Calories 323,64

Calories From Fat (81%) 261,85

% Daily Value

Total Fat 29,66g 46%

Saturated Fat 4,15g 21%

Cholesterol 22,68mg 8%

Sodium 232,58mg 10%

Potassium 464,37mg 13%

Total Carbohydrates 12,78g 4%

Fiber 3,83g 15%

Sugar 5,37g

Protein 4,58g 9%

Beef and Vegetables Stew

Ingredients

2 lbs beef boneless cut in pieces

3 Tbsp olive oil

3 cups vegetable broth

3 cups water

1 tsp parsley, dried

1 tsp rosemary, dried

2 yellow bell peppers, seeds removed and cut into halves

3 carrots, sliced

3 celery stalks, sliced

1 large onion, finely diced

2 tsp flour, white, all-purpose

2 tsp cold water

1 tsp pepper black, freshly ground

Instructions

1. In a large saucepan, heat the olive oil over moderate heat.
2. Sauté the beef cubes until brown from all sides for about 5 minutes; stir occasionally.
3. Pour the broth and the water into the pot.
4. Season the rosemary, parsley, and pepper.
5. Bring to boil and reduce the heat; cover the saucepan and simmer for 55 - 60 minutes.
6. Add the peppers, carrots, celery, and onion and stir well.
7. Dissolve the flour in 2 teaspoons cold water and pour it in the saucepan; stir.
8. Cover and simmer for further 10 minutes. (Internal temperature of meat has to be at least 145 degrees Fahrenheit).
9. Allow cooling on room temperature.
10. Store in a freezer-safe container, and keep in a freezer.

Servings: 8

Preparation Time: 1 hour and 15 minutes

Nutrition Facts

Serving size: 1/8 of a recipe (11.3 ounces)

Percent daily values based on the Reference Daily Intake (RDI) for a 2000 calorie diet.

Nutrition information calculated from recipe ingredients.

Amount per Serving

Calories 438,93

Calories From Fat (63%) 276,24

% Daily Value

Total Fat 30,15g 46%

Saturated Fat 10,49g 52%

Cholesterol 85,97mg 29%

Sodium 724,13mg 30%

Potassium 684,94mg 20%

Total Carbohydrates 17,61g 6%

Fiber 2,97g 12%

Sugar 2,4g

Protein 23,31g 47%

Braised Green Beans with Tomato and Parsley

Ingredients

1 1/2 lbs green beans, cleaned

1 large potato

2 carrots cut in rings

1 onion finely diced

1/2 lb grated tomato

1 cup of chopped parsley

2 cups of hot water

1/2 cup olive oil

Sea salt and black ground pepper to taste

Instructions

1. In a large saucepan heat the olive oil.
2. Sauté the onion with a pinch of salt, potatoes, and carrot for 5 minutes, stirring occasionally.
3. Add the green beans and cook for about 10 minutes.
4. Add the grated tomatoes and warm water; bring to boil and stir well.
5. Reduce heat to low, cover and cook for 20 minutes.
6. Season salt and pepper, add chopped parsley and stir well. Cover and cook for 15 minutes more.
7. Store soup in freezer-safe container or bag, and keep in a freezer.

Servings: 6

Preparation Time: 1 hour and 5 minutes

Nutrition Facts

Serving size: 1/6 of a recipe (10.4 ounces)

Percent daily values based on the Reference Daily Intake (RDI) for a 2000 calorie diet.

Nutrition information calculated from recipe ingredients.

Amount per Serving

Calories 238,9

Calories From Fat (68%) 162,46

% Daily Value

Total Fat 18,4g 28%

Saturated Fat 2,58g 13%

Cholesterol 0mg 0%

Sodium 33,71mg 1%

Potassium 513,22mg 15%

Total Carbohydrates 18,07g 6%

Fiber 5g 20%

Sugar 6,12g

Protein 3,32g 7%

Braised Pork with Eggplants and Peppers

Ingredients

2 lbs eggplants cut into slices

1/2 lb pork cut into cubes

1/2 cup water

1 cup olive oil

2 onions finely chopped

1/2 Tbsp of tomato paste (without salt added)

2 red sweet bell peppers

1/2 tsp sea salt

Instructions

1. Clean and cut eggplants into large slices.
2. Rub the eggplant slices with sea salt and place in a colander to drain.
3. Place the eggplant in a colander, rinse with cold water and drain; set aside.
4. Heat the oil in a large frying skillet over medium-high heat.
5. Sauté the pork with a little salt for about 5 - 6 minutes; stir occasionally.
6. Add all remaining ingredients (except eggplant) and bring to boil.
7. Reduce the heat to medium-low and let simmer for 30 - 40 minutes.
8. In a meantime, fry the eggplants and place them on a kitchen paper to drain for 10 minutes.
9. Finally, add eggplants to the frying pan with eggplant that and cook all together for 5 minutes.
10. Allow cooling on room temperature.
11. Store soup in freezer-safe container or bag, and keep in a freezer.

Servings: 6

Preparation Time: 1 hour and 5 minutes

Nutrition Facts

Serving size: 1/6 of a recipe (11.8 ounces)

Percent daily values based on the Reference Daily Intake (RDI)

for a 2000 calorie diet.

Nutrition information calculated from recipe ingredients.

Amount per Serving

Calories 552,87

Calories From Fat (85%) 469,96

% Daily Value

Total Fat 52,86g 81%

Saturated Fat 10,51g 53%

Cholesterol 24,74mg 8%

Sodium 348,03mg 15%

Potassium 588,95mg 17%

Total Carbohydrates 15,68g 5%

Fiber 6,87g 27%

Sugar 7,36g

Protein 6,69g 13%

Braised Squid and Potato Stew

Ingredients

2 lbs of potatoes

1 lemon juice and zest

2 Tbsp of olive oil

1/2 cup of white wine

2 cans (6 oz) cans calamari (squid)

1 onion finely chopped

Salt and ground pepper to taste

Chopped fresh parsley, for serving

Instructions

1. Clean the potatoes and cut into cubes.
2. Boil potatoes with salt, pepper and juice from 1 lemon until they soften (12-15 minutes). Drain and set aside.
3. Heat the oil in a large frying skillet over moderate-strong heat.
4. Add potatoes and cook for 2-3 minutes until they get a nice color.
5. Pour the wine and simmer for 1-2 minutes; add the squid, chopped onion, salt and pepper.
6. Mix and cook until the sauce is tied for 1-2 minutes.
7. Allow to cool on room temperature; store in a freezer-safe container, and keep in a freezer.
8. Serve with chopped parsley, lemon zest and olive oil.

Servings: 6

Preparation Time: 30 minutes

Nutrition Facts

Serving size: 1/6 of a recipe (9.6 ounces)

Percent daily values based on the Reference Daily Intake (RDI) for a 2000 calorie diet.

Nutrition information calculated from recipe ingredients.

Amount per Serving

Calories 234,67

Calories From Fat (21%) 48,32

% Daily Value

Total Fat 5,47g 8%

Saturated Fat 0,88g 4%

Cholesterol 132,11mg 44%

Sodium 84,98mg 4%

Potassium 836,36mg 24%

Total Carbohydrates 31,58g 11%

Fiber 4,12g 16%

Sugar 2,24g

Protein 12,25g 25%

Chicken and Peppers Risotto

Ingredients

1 chicken breast, boneless

4 cups water

2 Tbsp butter (grass fed), softened

1 cup of Basmati rice

1/2 red pepper

1/2 yellow pepper

1/2 orange pepper

Salt and black ground pepper to taste

Instructions

1. Boil the chicken in a pot with 4 cups of salted water for

20-25 minutes. Keep the broth for later.
2. Remove the chicken from the pot and cut into small pieces.
3. Heat the butter in a frying pan or wok; sauté chopped peppers for 2-3 minutes.
4. Add the rice and cook for another 2-3 minutes.
5. Add some broth and cook the rice and peppers on low heat for 15 minutes.
6. Once the rice absorbs the broth, add the chicken, salt and pepper to taste.
7. Cook until the rice is completely ready.
8. Allow cooling on room temperature.
9. Store risotto in a freezer-safe container or bag, and keep in a freezer.

Servings: 4

Preparation Time: 50 minutes

Nutrition Facts

Serving size: 1/4 of a recipe (7 ounces)

Percent daily values based on the Reference Daily Intake (RDI) for a 2000 calorie diet.

Nutrition information calculated from recipe ingredients.

Amount per Serving

Calories 302,75

Calories From Fat (22%) 65,72

% Daily Value

Total Fat 7,43g 11%

Saturated Fat 4g 20%

Cholesterol 53,03mg 18%

Sodium 225,02mg 9%

Potassium 335,12mg 10%

Total Carbohydrates 40,38g 13%

Fiber 0,93g 4%

Sugar 1,53g

Protein 16,5g 33%

Creamy Green Split Peas Chowder

Ingredients

1 cup green split peas, rinsed

1 Tbsp Italian seasoning mix

4 cups water

1 cup fresh cream

1/2 cup of cooked corn

1/2 cup of chopped onion

1/2 cup fresh chopped cilantro

Salt and pepper to taste

Instructions

1. Combine peas, Italian seasonings, and water in a medium pot. Cook on medium-high heat and bring to a boil.
2. Reduce heat, cover, and simmer 45 minutes, or until peas are tender.
3. Stir in corn, onion, and the salt and pepper: simmer for 10 minutes or until onions are tender.
4. Stir in the chopped cilantro, stir and cook for further 3 minutes; stir well.
5. Transfer chowder in a blender, add cream and blend until smooth.
6. Store in a freezer-safe container, and keep in a freezer.

Servings: 4

Preparation Time: 1 hour and 5 minutes

Nutrition Facts

Serving size: 1/4 of a recipe (13.2 ounces)

Percent daily values based on the Reference Daily Intake (RDI) for a 2000 calorie diet.

Nutrition information calculated from recipe ingredients.

Amount per Serving

Calories 445,8

Calories From Fat (45%) 199,32

% Daily Value

Total Fat 22,71g 35%

Saturated Fat 13,79g 69%

Cholesterol 81,52mg 27%

Sodium 188,16mg 8%

Potassium 589,17mg 17%

Total Carbohydrates 48,63g 16%

Fiber 13,35g 53%

Sugar 4,85g

Protein 13,76g 28%

Halibut and Celery Casserole

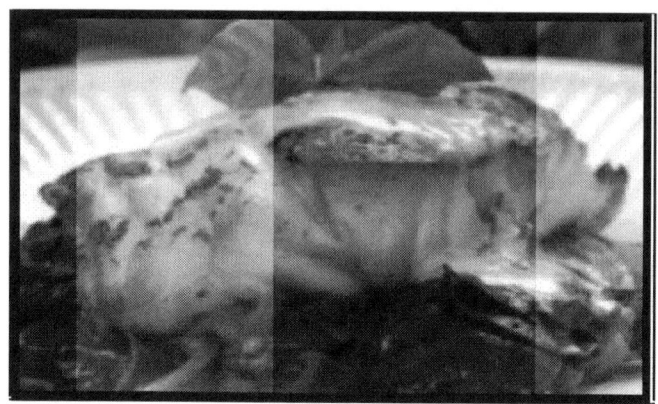

Ingredients

3 lbs of Halibut fish (or sea bass)

3 lbs of celery

1/2 cup white wine

1 cup of olive oil

Fresh juice of 1 lemon; (about 2 Tbsp)

Salt and black pepper freshly ground

Instructions

1. Cut the fish into thick slices and season with salt and pepper.
2. Wash and clean the celery and finely chop.
3. Place the pieces of celery in a large saucepan.
4. Place the fish slices over the celery.

5. Pour olive oil and lemon juice and cook over high heat until boil, about 6 - 8 minutes.
6. Pour the wine and let it evaporate for 5-6 minutes.
7. Taste and adjust salt and pepper to taste.
8. Allow cooling on room temperature.
9. Store in a freezer-safe container, and keep in a freezer.

Servings: 8

Preparation Time: 30 minutes

Nutrition Facts

Serving size: 1/8 of a recipe (13 ounces)

Percent daily values based on the Reference Daily Intake (RDI) for a 2000 calorie diet.

Nutrition information calculated from recipe ingredients.

Amount per Serving

Calories 436,61

Calories From Fat (59%) 257,12

% Daily Value

Total Fat 29,05g 45%

Saturated Fat 4,2g 21%

Cholesterol 62,94mg 21%

Sodium 227,62mg 9%

Potassium 1284,86mg 37%

Total Carbohydrates 6,07g 2%

Fiber 2,79g 11%

Sugar 3,44g

Protein 34,2g 68%

Japanese Style Mushroom Shrimp Stew

Ingredients

1/4 cup olive oil

3/4 lb fresh mushrooms (portabella and shiitakes) sliced

2 cups fresh celery, sliced

2 green peppers, sliced

2 onions finely chopped

1/2 cup tamari (naturally fermented soy sauce)

2 Tbsp brown sugar - (packed)

1 lb frozen shrimp, peeled and deveined

1/2 cup beef broth (homemade, if available)

Instructions

1. Heat the oil in a large skillet over medium-high heat. Sauté celery, green peppers and onions, with a little salt, for about 5 minutes.
2. Add all remaining ingredients.
3. Reduce heat and simmer for about 12 - 15 minutes longer or until shrimp turn pink.
4. Taste and adjust seasonings to taste.
5. Allow cooling on room temperature.
6. Store in a freezer-safe container, and keep in a freezer.

Servings: 6

Preparation Time: 25 minutes

Nutrition Facts

Serving size: 1/6 of a recipe (11.2 ounces)

Percent daily values based on the Reference Daily Intake (RDI) for a 2000 calorie diet.

Nutrition information calculated from recipe ingredients.

Amount per Serving

Calories 212,44

Calories From Fat (43%) 91,25

% Daily Value

Total Fat 10,32g 16%

Saturated Fat 1,46g 7%

Cholesterol 95,46mg 32%

Sodium 1226,17mg 51%

Potassium 571,64mg 16%

Total Carbohydrates 16,9g 6%

Fiber 3,05g 12%

Sugar 9,49g

Protein 14,53g 29%

Lamb Fricassee with Lettuce

Ingredients

2 lb lamb boneless, cut into pieces

6 green onions chopped

4 garlic cloves

3 lettuce head chopped

1/3 cup of olive oil

2 free-range eggs

2 - 3 lemons, juice

1 bunch of dill

Salt and ground black pepper

Instructions

1. Heat the oil in a frying skillet and sauté the lamb pieces for 2- 3 minutes.
2. Add water, dill, and the salt and pepper; let it boil for about 45 minutes.
3. Add the garlic, lettuces and continue to cook for a further 10 minutes.
4. In a meantime, beat the eggs with a pinch of salt. Then, pour the lemon juice and stir well.
5. Pour the egg-lemon mixture into pot very slowly, stir well and boil for 1 minute.
6. Taste and adjust seasonings.
7. Allow cooling on room temperature.
8. Store in a freezer-safe glass container, and keep in a freezer.

Servings: 8

Preparation Time: 1 hour and 5 minutes

Nutrition Facts

Serving size: 1/8 of a recipe (14 ounces)

Percent daily values based on the Reference Daily Intake (RDI) for a 2000 calorie diet.

Nutrition information calculated from recipe ingredients.

Amount per Serving

Calories 374,44

Calories From Fat (63%) 234,52

% Daily Value

Total Fat 26,25g 40%

Saturated Fat 8,31g 42%

Cholesterol 122,48mg 41%

Sodium 103,64mg 4%

Potassium 946,88mg 27%

Total Carbohydrates 10,19g 3%

Fiber 5,31g 21%

Sugar 3,5g

Protein 25,89g 52%

Lemony Artichokes with Fresh Dill

Ingredients

1 lb frozen artichoke

2 carrots cut into slices

2 potatoes cut into cubes

1 cup of olive oil

1 cup onion, finely chopped

3 Tbsp fresh dill finely chopped

2 lemons, the juice

2 organics eggs beaten

Salt and freshly ground black pepper to taste

Instructions

1. Heat the oil in a large frying skillet and sauté potatoes, carrots, and onions with a pinch of salt.
2. Add artichokes and sauté for 5 to 6 minutes.
3. Add as much water as you need to cover the artichokes; season with the salt and pepper and boil over medium heat for 50 minutes.
4. Remove from heat and allow cool on room temperature; for 20 minutes covered with a lid.
5. Beat eggs with the lemon juice and pour very slowly over artichokes; give a good stir.
6. Remove the skillet on heat again, and cook for 1 to 2 minutes.
7. Sprinkle with dill and allow cool on room temperature.
8. Store in a freezer-safe container, and keep in a freezer.

Servings: 6

Preparation Time: 1 hour and 5 minutes

Inactive Time: 20 minutes

Nutrition Facts

Serving size: 1/6 of a recipe (9.7 ounces)

Percent daily values based on the Reference Daily Intake (RDI) for a 2000 calorie diet.

Nutrition information calculated from recipe ingredients.

Amount per Serving

Calories 453,28

Calories From Fat (74%) 335,02

% Daily Value

Total Fat 37,9g 58%

Saturated Fat 5,54g 28%

Cholesterol 62mg 21%

Sodium 168,37mg 7%

Potassium 696,76mg 20%

Total Carbohydrates 25,74g 9%

Fiber 6,7g 27%

Sugar 3,45g

Protein 6,59g 13%

Marinated and Grilled Pork Cutlets

Ingredients

4 pork cutlets

2 large lemons freshly squeezed

1 cup fresh orange juice

2 Tbsp fresh parsley finely chopped

10 twigs of coriander

1 tsp ground caraway

3 Tbsp olive oil

Salt and ground black pepper

Instructions

1. Place the pork cutlets in a large resealable bag along with

lemon juice, orange juice, coriander, parsley, caraway, olive oil, and salt and pepper.
2. Refrigerate it at least 4 hours, or overnight.
3. Remove the pork cutlets from marinade and pat dry on kitchen towel.
4. Preheat the grill (any).
5. Place pork chops on grill grate and grill for 10 minutes per side (or to taste).
6. Allow cooling on room temperature.
7. Store in a freezer-safe glass or plastic container, and keep in a freezer.

Servings: 4

Preparation Time: 35 minutes

Nutrition Facts

Serving size: 1/4 of a recipe (7.7 ounces)

Percent daily values based on the Reference Daily Intake (RDI) for a 2000 calorie diet.

Nutrition information calculated from recipe ingredients.

Amount per Serving

Calories 288,25

Calories From Fat (47%) 135,14

% Daily Value

Total Fat 15,18g 23%

Saturated Fat 3,13g 16%

Cholesterol 93,56mg 31%

Sodium 71,55mg 3%

Potassium 642,35mg 18%

Total Carbohydrates 4,68g 2%

Fiber 0,41g 2%

Sugar 2,57g

Protein 32,19g 64%

Pork Fillets with Mustard Mushrooms Sauce

Ingredients

1/2 cup olive oil

6 pork fillets

1 dry onion finely chopped

2 cloves garlic chopped

1/2 lb fresh whole mushrooms small

1 glass of dry white wine

Sea salt and black pepper

2 cups warm water

Fresh oregano finely chopped

Fresh basil finely chopped

2 tsp Stone-ground Mustard

2 Tbsp almond flour

1/2 cup warm water

Instructions

1. Heat the oil in a deep frying pan with a lid.
2. Sauté the pork fillets for 5-6 minutes from both sides.
3. Add the onion, garlic, and the mushrooms and sauté for 5 minutes; stir.
4. Pour the wine, add salt, pepper, warm water, cover the pan and cook for about 30-40 minutes over medium heat. (Cooking depends on the thickness of the pork).
5. Sprinkle the oregano and basil, the mustard dissolved in 1/2 cup of water and shake the pan to incorporate all ingredients well.
6. Simmer with an open lid for 5 minutes.
7. Allow cooling on room temperature.
8. Store in a freezer-safe container, and keep in a freezer.

Servings: 6

Preparation Time: 55 minutes

Nutrition Facts

Serving size: 1/6 of a recipe (9.6 ounces)

Percent daily values based on the Reference Daily Intake (RDI)

for a 2000 calorie diet.

Nutrition information calculated from recipe ingredients.

Amount per Serving

Calories 401,93

Calories From Fat (82%) 327,79

% Daily Value

Total Fat 36,84g 57%

Saturated Fat 8,33g 42%

Cholesterol 25,84mg 9%

Sodium 343,73mg 14%

Potassium 286,97mg 8%

Total Carbohydrates 5,49g 2%

Fiber 1,18g 5%

Sugar 2,16g

Protein 6,58g 13%

WARM SALADS

◆ ◆ ◆

Beetroot Leaves Salad with Broccoli and Sheep Cheese

Ingredients

1 lbs beetroot leaves

1/2 medium broccoli, cut into floweret

2 cloves of garlic, sliced

1 large dry toast, crumbled

1/2 cup of olive oil

3 Tbsp of lemon juice

9 oz sheep cheese, crumbled

1 tsp sweet paprika

2 tsp toasted sesame seeds

Salt, freshly ground pepper

Instructions

1. In a saucepan, heat salted water to boil and cook beet-root leaves for about 2-3 minutes, just until softened.
2. Remove them with a pierced ladle and leave them in a strainer to drain.
3. In the same boiling water, boil the broccoli for about 5 minutes, until it is slightly soaked, remove it with a pierced spoon and place it in a salad bowl.
4. In a large frying pan, heat the olive oil and sauté the garlic for about one minute.
5. Add the beetroot leaves, season with the salt and pepper, and sauté for about 1-2 minutes; remove from the heat and place with the broccoli.
6. Sprinkle with the salt and pepper and add crumbled hard toast.
7. In the same pan heat the oil, add paprika and lemon and heat them for about 1/2 - 1 minute.
8. Remove from the fire and stir sheep cheese, sesame, and the salt and pepper to taste; mix well.
9. Pour the cheese mixture in a salad bowl, and gently stir.
10. Keep refrigerated in a closed container up to three days.

Servings: 4

Preparation Time: 20 minutes

Nutrition Facts

Serving size: 1/4 of a recipe (9 ounces)

Percent daily values based on the Reference Daily Intake (RDI) for a 2000 calorie diet.

Nutrition information calculated from recipe ingredients.

Amount per Serving

Calories 488,45

Calories From Fat (75%) 452,72

% Daily Value

Total Fat 51,41g 79%

Saturated Fat 19,75g 99%

Cholesterol 66,98mg 22%

Sodium 329,79mg 14%

Total Carbohydrates 16,13g 5%

Fiber 4,27g 17%

Sugar 2,57g

Protein 24,01g 48%

Golden Vegetables with Balsamic Vinegar

Ingredients

1 eggplant

3 zucchinis

1 leek

1 large onion

4 peppers (red, green, yellow ...)

2 large tomatoes

Salt and ground black pepper to taste

1 tsp oregano

1/2 cup olive oil

1 Tbsp balsamic vinegar

Instructions

1. Preheat the oven to 350 F/175 C.
2. Cut the vegetables in pieces and place in a greased baking pan.
3. Season with the oregano, olive oil and the salt and pepper to taste.
4. Stir lightly and add balsamic vinegar and toss.
5. Bake for 65 - 70 minutes.
6. Let cool on room temperature.
7. Store in a container and refrigerate for 3 to 4 days or store in a freezer-safe container, and keep in a freezer.

Servings: 8

Preparation Time: 1 hour and 10 minutes

Nutrition Facts

Serving size: 1/8 of a recipe (13.2 ounces)

Percent daily values based on the Reference Daily Intake (RDI) for a 2000 calorie diet.

Nutrition information calculated from recipe ingredients.

Amount per Serving

Calories 205,86

Calories From Fat (61%) 126,18

% Daily Value

Total Fat 14,3g 22%

Saturated Fat 2,01g 10%

Cholesterol 0mg 0%

Sodium 248,91mg 10%

Potassium 772,89mg 22%

Total Carbohydrates 18,69g 6%

Fiber 6,3g 25%

Sugar 10,68g

Protein 3,59g 7%

Greek Salad - Horta, Asparagus and Cheese Sauce

Ingredients

2 lbs of Greek Horta - amaranth or mustard greens cleaned, washed, coarsely

1 bunch of asparagus green (about 10 -12 pieces), cleaned and cut 4 pieces

Salt and ground black pepper to taste

For the sauce

1/2 cup of olive oil

1 Tbsp rosemary leaves, finely chopped

1 tsp hot dried paprika

1 cup mascarpone or ricotta cheese

1 clove of garlic, cleaned finely minced

Instructions

1. Boil salted water in a saucepan with plenty of salted boiling water.
2. Boil the greens and asparagus for about 7 to 10 minutes.
3. Drain well and put in a large bowl.

Warm sauce:

1. In a frying pan heat the olive oil and heat the garlic over medium heat.
2. Add the cheese, rosemary leaves, and hot dried paprika salt and freshly ground pepper; stir well.
3. Stir for 15 - 20 seconds and remove from the heat.
4. Pour hot cheese salad over the greens and asparagus.
5. Let it cool, store in a container with a lid and refrigerate up to 3 days.

Servings: 6

Preparation Time: 20 minutes

Nutrition Facts

Serving size: 1/6 of a recipe (8 ounces)

Percent daily values based on the Reference Daily Intake (RDI)

for a 2000 calorie diet.

Nutrition information calculated from recipe ingredients.

Amount per Serving

Calories 260,41

Calories From Fat (73%) 190,9

% Daily Value

Total Fat 21,63g 33%

Saturated Fat 4,54g 23%

Cholesterol 12,71mg 4%

Sodium 187,04mg 8%

Potassium 631,66mg 18%

Total Carbohydrates 10,57g 4%

Fiber 5,51g 22%

Sugar 2,89g

Protein 9,2g 18%

Warm Salad with Artichokes, Peas and Sour Dressing

Ingredients

4 artichokes (cooked)

2 cups peas (cooked)

4 boiled eggs (hard)

4 green onions finely chopped

2 Tbsp fresh dill finely chopped

2 Tbsp fresh mint finely chopped

3 Tbsp capers

10 olives

Dressing

1/2 cup olive oil

1 Tbsp lemon juice

2 Tbsp white vinegar

1 boiled egg yolk

Sea salt and freshly ground black pepper

Instructions

1. Fill a large pot with lightly salted water; bring to boiling.
2. Add artichokes and return water to boiling.
3. Reduce heat; simmer, covered, for about 20 to 30 minutes.
4. Remove from the water and let cook for 10 minutes.
5. Cut artichokes in quarters and place in a salad bowl.
6. Add the peas, eggs cut into four, spring onions, dill, mint, the caper, and olives.

For the dressing:

1. Melt the egg yolk with the fork, season salt, pepper, lemon juice, and vinegar; stir well.
2. Pour some olive oil and whisk until becomes creamy.
3. Pour the dressing over the salad and toss to combine well.
4. Refrigerate in a covered container for three days or store in a freezer-safe container and keep in a freezer.

Servings: 6

Preparation Time: 50 minutes

Nutrition Facts

Serving size: 1/6 of a recipe (8.7 ounces)

Percent daily values based on the Reference Daily Intake (RDI) for a 2000 calorie diet.

Nutrition information calculated from recipe ingredients.

Amount per Serving

Calories 474,34

Calories From Fat (43%) 216,4

% Daily Value

Total Fat 24,45g 38%

Saturated Fat 4,23g 21%

Cholesterol 171,45mg 57%

Sodium 208,97mg 9%

Total Carbohydrates 50,92g 17%

Fiber 21,92g 88%

Sugar 6,85g

Protein 24,4g 49%

Warm Salad with Avocado

Ingredients

2 Tbsp olive oil

1 small onion

2 cloves of garlic

1 Tbsp fresh thyme finely chopped

3 zucchini

Black ground pepper to taste

1 lemon (zest and juice)

1 large avocado

Instructions

1. Heat some olive oil in a frying pan.
2. Sauté the garlic and onion and cook until soft, for about 4 - 5 minutes.
3. Add zucchinis and cook for about 3 minutes or until they are tender.
4. Add the lemon zest, thyme and pepper and mix for a few minutes.
5. In a deep dish, pour the lemon juice with the avocado.
6. Add them to the frying pan and cook over low heat until all ingredients soft.
7. Cool on room temperature; properly stored in a refrigerator it can last up to 3 - 4 days.
8. Also, you can store salad it in a freezer-safe container and keep in a freezer.

Servings: 4

Preparation Time: 20 minutes

Nutrition Facts

Serving size: 1/4 of a recipe (9. 7 ounces)

Percent daily values based on the Reference Daily Intake (RDI) for a 2000 calorie diet.

Nutrition information calculated from recipe ingredients.

Amount per Serving

Calories 181,66

Calories From Fat (67%) 121,14

% Daily Value

Total Fat 14,07g 22%

Saturated Fat 2,03g 10%

Cholesterol 0mg 0%

Sodium 18,12mg < 1%

Potassium 714,02mg 20%

Total Carbohydrates 14,54g 5%

Fiber 5,43g 22%

Sugar 6,07g

Protein 3,35g 7%

Warm Salad with Green Beans, Bacon & Potatoes

Ingredients

1 lb small potatoes, peeled and cut in half

4 slices of bacon cut lengthwise

1/2 lb green beans

2 Tbsp olive oil

2 Tbsp fresh lemon juice

2 cloves of garlic, minced

Salt and ground pepper, to taste

Instructions

1. In a saucepan, put the potatoes and cover them with salted water.
2. Boil the potatoes for 10-15 minutes until they tender; drain.
3. In a large non-stick pan, heat olive oil over moderate heat.
4. Sauté potatoes, garlic, and the salt pepper.
5. Cook the potatoes for about 5 minutes until golden brown.
6. Remove from the frying pan and set aside.
7. In the same frying pan, fry the bacon for about 3 minutes until brown and crispy.
8. Add the green beans and continue to cook for about 4 minutes, stirring occasionally until the beans are crispy.
9. Add the potatoes, lemon juice for extra flavor, season with the salt and pepper and gently stir.
10. Store your salad in a container and refrigerated up to 4 days.

Servings: 5

Preparation Time: 40 minutes

Nutrition Facts

Serving size: 1/5 of a recipe (6.7 ounces)

Percent daily values based on the Reference Daily Intake (RDI) for a 2000 calorie diet.

Nutrition information calculated from recipe ingredients.

Amount Per Serving

Calories 274,01

Calories From Fat (63%) 172,83

% Daily Value

Total Fat 19,29g 30%

Saturated Fat 5,35g 27%

Cholesterol 20,67mg 7%

Sodium 261,77mg 11%

Potassium 552,02mg 16%

Total Carbohydrates 20,03g 7%

Fiber 3,26g 13%

Sugar 2,35g

Protein 6,29g 13%

PIZZA

◆ ◆ ◆

Angelo Bianco Pizza

Ingredients

1 cup flour white, all-purpose

1/2 cup of water

1 tsp of yeast

2 Tbsp of olive oil

1 tsp of sugar

1/2 Tbsp salt

Topping:

3/4 cup of grated Parmesan

3/4 cup mozzarella crumbled

1 tsp dried oregano

Salt and black ground pepper

Instructions

1. Dissolve yeast in warm water and add to flour, olive oil, sugar, and salt.
2. Knead the dough about 12 minutes; cover and leave in a warm place to rise for an hour.
3. Preheat the oven at 400F/200 C.
4. Roll the dough in a thin sheet.
5. Spread the dough in a pizza pan and brush with the oil.
6. Sprinkle grated Parmesan and Mozzarella slices.
7. Season with the salt, pepper and sprinkle with dried oregano.
8. Place pizza pan in the oven and bake for about 15 minutes.
9. Let it cool and slice.
10. Wrap every pizza slice in aluminum foil and place in a plastic bag.
11. Freeze pizza up to 3 months.

Servings: 4

Preparation Time: 30 minutes

Inactive Time: 1 hour

Nutrition Facts

Serving size: 1/4 of a recipe (4.8 ounces)

Percent daily values based on the Reference Daily Intake (RDI) for a 2000 calorie diet.

Nutrition information calculated from recipe ingredients.

Amount per Serving

Calories 325,4

Calories From Fat (44%) 144,71

% Daily Value

Total Fat 16,45g 25%

Saturated Fat 6,74g 34%

Cholesterol 32,34mg 11%

Sodium 1314,21mg 55%

Potassium 92,5mg 3%

Total Carbohydrates 27,01g 9%

Fiber 1,27g 5%

Sugar 1,6g

Protein 16,88g 34

Delicious Greek Pizza

Ingredients

1 pizza dough

2 Tbsp tomato sauce

1/2 cup grated mozzarella

1/2 cup Gruyere cheese grated

4 slices smoked ham

Few rocket leaves

1/4 cup olive oil

1 Tbsp little oregano

Sauce

1 1/2 lbs fresh tomato, peeled and deseeded

2 cloves garlic

1 tsp sugar

1/4 cup fresh basil (chopped)

1 tsp tomato paste

1 pinch of dried oregano

Instructions

1. Preheat the oven to 400 F/220 C.
2. Sprinkle a working surface with the flour.
3. Open the pizza dough sheet on the floured surface.
4. Apply the sauce on the surface, sprinkle with the oregano, add the cheese and place pizza on a pizza pan.
5. Bake for 20-25 minutes or until the dough turns brown and the cheeses melt.
6. Remove pizza from the oven and add the smoked ham and the rocket, and sprinkle it with a few drops of olive oil.
7. Let it cool on room temperature and cut into 8 pieces.
8. Wrap the pizza slices in aluminum foil and place in a plastic bag.
9. Freeze for up to 2 months.

Sauce

1. Cut the tomatoes in the middle and remove the seeds and finely chop.
2. Place all the ingredients of the sauce in a deep saucepan and let them boil.
3. Once they start to boil, stir with a wooden spoon, pressing the tomatoes to melt. Reduce the heat and simmer the sauce for 20, stirring occasionally.
4. Season with the salt and pepper to taste and stir.
5. Keep the sauce refrigerated for 5 days in airtight container.
6. Also, you can freeze the sauce in a freezer-safe container up to 3 months.

Servings: 8

Preparation Time: 55 minutes

Nutrition Facts

Serving size: 1/8 of a recipe (6.1 ounces)

Percent daily values based on the Reference Daily Intake (RDI) for a 2000 calorie diet.

Nutrition information calculated from recipe ingredients.

Amount Per Serving

Calories 254,91

Calories From Fat (42%) 107,53

% Daily Value

Total Fat 12,15g 19%

Saturated Fat 3,39g 17%

Cholesterol 16,14mg 5%

Sodium 190,35mg 8%

Potassium 373,11mg 11%

Total Carbohydrates 27,29g 9%

Fiber 2,49g 10%

Sugar 3,22g

Protein 10,11g 20%

Double Cheese Turkey Pizza

Ingredients

1 pizza crust prepared

1 can (15 oz) Pizza Tomato Sauce

1/2 cup garlic paste

8 oz smoked turkey shredded

1/2 cup shredded Muenster cheese

1/2 cup shredded Provolone cheese

1/2 tsp red pepper flakes

Instructions

1. Preheat oven to 400°F/200 C.
2. Spread garlic paste evenly over pizza crust. Add shredded turkey over salsa.
3. Top pizza with Muenster cheese and shredded Provolone cheese. Sprinkle with red pepper flakes.
4. Bake for 15 - 20 minutes or until cheese is melted and golden brown.
5. When ready, let it cool and slice.
6. Wrap each slice of pizza in aluminum foil, place in a plastic bag and freeze for up to 2 months.

Servings: 8

Preparation Time: 25 minutes

Nutrition Facts

Serving size: 1/8 of a recipe (5.9 ounces)

Percent daily values based on the Reference Daily Intake (RDI) for a 2000 calorie diet.

Nutrition information calculated from recipe ingredients.

Amount per Serving

Calories 266,57

Calories From Fat (28%) 75,37

% Daily Value

Total Fat 8,35g 13%

Saturated Fat 3,32g 17%

Cholesterol 31,28mg 10%

Sodium 783,12mg 33%

Potassium 268,17mg 8%

Total Carbohydrates 29,94g 10%

Fiber 0,8g 3%

Sugar 2,34g

Protein 17g 34%

Easy Homemade Pizza

Ingredients

1 1/4 cups milk

1/4 cup of olive oil

1/2 tsp salt

1/2 tsp sugar

1 envelop instant yeast

1 lb of flour

Topping

1 cup tomato pizza sauce

4 slices ham, cut in cubes

A handful of baby spinach

1 cup grated Parmesan cheese

Instructions

1. Preheat the oven to 400F.
2. In the lukewarm milk, add crumbled yeast, sugar and a teaspoon of flour; stir for 30 - 45 seconds.
3. Add flour in a deep container and add yeast, milk olive oil, salt, and sugar.
4. Knead the dough for 10 - 12 minutes or until a sticky dough forms.
5. Place pizza dough in a pizza pan; pour the tomato sauce, ham, mushrooms, baby spinach, and grated Parmesan cheese, and black olives (optional).
6. Place in oven and bake for 15 minutes.
7. Let it cool and slice.
8. Wrap every pizza slice in aluminum foil and place in a plastic bag. Freeze pizza up to 3 months.

Servings: 8

Preparation Time: 35 minutes

Nutrition Facts

Serving size: 1/8 of a recipe (6.7 ounces)

Percent daily values based on the Reference Daily Intake (RDI) for a 2000 calorie diet.

Nutrition information calculated from recipe ingredients.

Amount per Serving

Calories 382,52

Calories From Fat (30%) 113,24

% Daily Value

Total Fat 12,84g 20%

Saturated Fat 4,03g 20%

Cholesterol 24,36mg 8%

Sodium 775,27mg 32%

Potassium 368,5mg 11%

Total Carbohydrates 48,33g 16%

Fiber 2,5g 10%

Sugar 3,81g

Protein 17,74g 35%

Four - Cheese and Rosemary Pizza

Ingredients

1 ready-made fresh pizza dough

1 cup of tomato sauce

1/2 cups grated Provolone

1/2 cup grated Parmesan

1/2 cup Mozzarella, coarse-grained

1/2 cup goat cheese

1 tsp dry rosemary

1 Tbsp cornstarch

Instructions

1. Preheat the oven to 400 ° F/ 220 ° C (air mode).
2. Sprinkle a pizza pan with corn-flour.
3. Open the dough and spread it on the pizza pan.
4. Spread the tomato sauce evenly over the dough and sprinkle with 4 kinds of cheese and rosemary.
5. Bake for about 15 - 17 minutes or until the cheese melts.
6. Let cool on room temperature and slice into 8 pieces.
7. Wrap each piece in aluminum foil and place in a plastic bag. Freeze up to 2 months.

Servings: 8

Preparation Time: 25 minutes

Nutrition Facts

Serving size: 1/8 of a recipe (4.4 ounces)

Percent daily values based on the Reference Daily Intake (RDI) for a 2000 calorie diet.

Nutrition information calculated from recipe ingredients.

Amount Per Serving

Calories 235,65

Calories From Fat (36%) 84,72

% Daily Value

Total Fat 9,6g 15%

Saturated Fat 5,55g 28%

Cholesterol 22,99mg 8%

Sodium 433,14mg 18%

Potassium 177,29mg 5%

Total Carbohydrates 24,46g 8%

Fiber 0,73g 3%

Sugar 1,62g

Protein 12,6g 25%

Italiana Cremini Funghi Pizza

Ingredients

3 cup fresh Cremini mushrooms, sliced

1 large bell pepper cut in slices

1 1/2 cups shredded Gruyere cheese

16 ounces pizza dough

1/2 cup grated Pecorino Romano cheese

3 Tbsp Italian salad dressing

2 Tbsp Fresh chopped parsley for garnishing

Instructions

1. Preheat oven to 450 degrees F/220C.
2. Cut mushrooms into thin slices, and cut bell pepper in thin strips.
3. Sprinkle shredded Gruyere cheese over pizza crust.
4. In a large bowl, combine mushrooms and the pepper strips, Parmesan and salad dressing until well blended.
5. Apply the mushrooms mixture over the pizza crust.
6. Sprinkle with grated Pecorino Romano cheese.
7. Bake until mushrooms are tender and cheese has melted, 10 to 12 minutes.
8. Top with chopped parsley, if desired.
9. Let it cool; slice and wrap every slice in aluminum foil, and place in a plastic bag.
10. Freeze for up to two months.

Servings: 8

Preparation Time: 25 minutes

Nutrition Facts

Serving size: 1/8 of a recipe (6 ounces)

Percent daily values based on the Reference Daily Intake (RDI) for a 2000 calorie diet.

Nutrition information calculated from recipe ingredients.

Amount per Serving

Calories 317,83

Calories From Fat (35%) 112,4

% Daily Value

Total Fat 12,58g 19%

Saturated Fat 4,63g 23%

Cholesterol 30,28mg 10%

Sodium 857,14mg 36%

Potassium 205,78mg 6%

Total Carbohydrates 36,1g 12%

Fiber 0,59g 2%

Sugar 6,59g

Protein 14,68g 29%

Peach and Pineapple Pepperoni Pizza

Ingredients

1 12-inch regular pizza crust

1/2 cup pizza sauce to taste

1 1/2 cups shredded Mozzarella cheese

1 large peach, sliced

1 cup pineapple chunks

2 oz sliced pepperoni (pork sausages seasoned with pepper)

Diced green peppers (optional)

Instructions

1. Preheat oven to 425 F/ 200C.
2. Spread pizza crust with sauce. Sprinkle with half the cheese.
3. Top with fruit slices and pepperoni sausage, then sprinkle with remaining cheese and the green pepper.
4. Place in a baking pan, and bake for 15 minutes or until heated through.
5. Remove from oven and cut into slices.
6. Wrap each slice in aluminum foil and place in a plastic bag.
7. Freeze for up to two months.

Servings: 8

Preparation Time: 35 minutes

Nutrition Facts

Serving size: 1/8 of a recipe (4.4 ounces)

Percent daily values based on the Reference Daily Intake (RDI) for a 2000 calorie diet.

Nutrition information calculated from recipe ingredients.

Amount Per Serving

Calories 226,41

Calories From Fat (38%) 85,79

% Daily Value

Total Fat 9,78g 15%

Saturated Fat 6,12g 31%

Cholesterol 39,06mg 13%

Sodium 727,21mg 30%

Potassium 193,64mg 6%

Total Carbohydrates 21,42g 7%

Fiber 1,14g 5%

Sugar 2,9g

Protein 13,08g 26%

Simple Margarita Pizza

Ingredients

1 1/2 cups of self-rising flour

1 cup Greek yogurt

1 tsp of oregano

5 Tbsp of tomato paste

2 Tbsp of ketchup

1 cup of grated mozzarella

1 cup grated Gouda

Instructions

1. Preheat the oven to 400 F/220C.
2. Line a pizza pan with the parchment paper.
3. In a bowl, stir the flour, yogurt, and 1/2 teaspoon oregano.
4. Knead until dough becomes a soft; make a ball.
5. Cut dough on 4 pieces.
6. On a floured surface, roll each piece with a rolling pin in a thin sheet.
7. Lay the sheets one by one, in a prepared pizza pan.
8. Stir the tomato paste with ketchup and oregano and pour over the dough.
9. Cover with shredded mozzarella and Gouda.
10. Place in the oven and bake for 15-20 minutes.
11. Remove from the oven and let cool on room temperature.
12. Wrap each pizza slice in aluminum foil and place in a plastic bag. Freeze up to three months.

Servings: 8

Preparation Time: 35 minutes

Nutrition Facts

Serving size: 1/8 of a recipe (4.4 ounces)

Percent daily values based on the Reference Daily Intake (RDI) for a 2000 calorie diet.

Nutrition information calculated from recipe ingredients.

Amount Per Serving

Calories 226,41

Calories From Fat (38%) 85,79

% Daily Value

Total Fat 9,78g 15%

Saturated Fat 6,12g 31%

Cholesterol 39,06mg 13%

Sodium 727,21mg 30%

Potassium 193,64mg 6%

Total Carbohydrates 21,42g 7%

Fiber 1,14g 5%

Sugar 2,9g

Protein 13,08g 26%

SOUPS/STEWS

♦ ♦ ♦

Avgolemono - Greek Traditional Chicken Soup

Ingredients

1 whole chicken, cleaned

8 cups water

2 small onions finely chopped

1 bunch of parsley finely chopped

1/4 cup fennel bulb, thinly sliced

1/2 tsp nutmeg grated

1/2 tsp allspice ground

¼ cup of bacon, crumbled

Salt and pepper to taste

2 lemons (juice)

4 organic eggs

Instructions

1. Place the chicken in a large pot with enough water.
2. Bring to boil, and then reduce heat to a gentle boil and cook for about 90 - 95 minutes or until chicken meat is falling off of the bone.
3. When ready, remove the chicken from the water (keep two cups of broth).
4. Add all remaining ingredients to the broth, (except lemon and eggs) and leave to boil for about 10 minutes.
5. Whisk eggs in a bowl with the pinch of salt; pour the lemon juice and stir well.
6. Slowly, pour the egg-lemon mixture in a broth; stir continuously.
7. Shred one chicken leg, and add meat in a soup.
8. Let soup cool on room temperature.
9. Store soup in freezer-safe container or bag, and keep in a freezer.

Servings: 8

Preparation Time: 1 hour and 35 minutes

Nutrition Facts

Serving size: 1/8 of a recipe (10.4 ounces)

Percent daily values based on the Reference Daily Intake (RDI)

for a 2000 calorie diet.

Nutrition information calculated from recipe ingredients.

Amount Per Serving

Calories 169,86

Calories From Fat (64%) 109,3

% Daily Value

Total Fat 12,17g 19%

Saturated Fat 3,87g 19%

Cholesterol 120,24mg 40%

Sodium 218,05mg 9%

Potassium 227,09mg 6%

Total Carbohydrates 5,86g 2%

Fiber 1,78g 7%

Sugar 1,8g

Protein 9,6g 19%

Chicken, Cabbage and Apple Stew

Ingredients

2 Tbsp chicken fat

1 chicken, cut in parts

1/4 cup apple cider vinegar

1/2 tsp nutmeg

6 whole cloves

6 apples, peeled, sliced

3 carrots, peeled, sliced

2 tsp Dijon mustard

1 cup shredded cabbage

1 3/4 cups chicken broth, warm

1/2 tsp salt and freshly ground black pepper to taste

Instructions

1. Heat the chicken fat in a large pot.
2. Add chicken and cook, turning on all sides, for about 10 minutes.
3. Sprinkle with nutmeg, salt, and pepper.
4. Spread mustard over chicken pieces; add warm broth, vinegar, cloves, and carrots; bring to a boil.
5. Cover, reduce heat to low and cook for 15 minutes.
6. Add apples and cook 5 minutes.
7. Add cabbage, give a good stir; cover and cook for further 10 -12 minutes.
8. Allow soup to cool; store soup in freezer-safe container or bag, and keep in a freezer.

Servings: 6

Preparation Time: 50 minutes

Nutrition Facts

Serving size: 1/6 of a recipe (14.8 ounces)

Percent daily values based on the Reference Daily Intake (RDI) for a 2000 calorie diet.

Nutrition information calculated from recipe ingredients.

Amount Per Serving

Calories 538,84

Calories From Fat (59%) 364,68

% Daily Value

Total Fat 40,51g 62%

Saturated Fat 11,61g 58%

Cholesterol 166,17mg 55%

Sodium 613,06mg 26%

Potassium 784,24mg 22%

Total Carbohydrates 22,05g 7%

Fiber 3,49g 14%

Sugar 15,61g

Protein 40,62g 81%

Creamy Basil Sun-Dried Tomato Soup

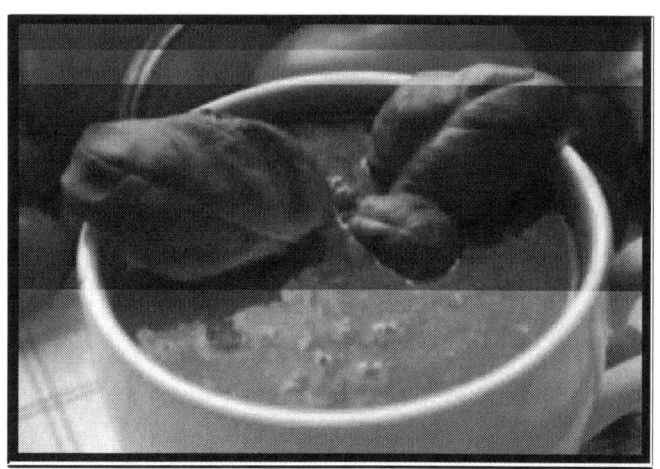

Ingredients

1/4 cup of olive oil

1 cup onion diced

1 cup sun-dried Tomatoes

1 lb fresh tomatoes in cubes

2 1/2 cup water

2 tsp apple cider vinegar

1 bunch of basil, finely chopped

1 cup milk (dairy or non-dairy)

Salt and ground pepper

1/2 tsp paprika sweet, powder

Instructions

1. Heat the olive oil in a pot over medium heat.
2. Sauté the onion and half sun-dried tomatoes with a pinch of salt for 3 - 4 minutes.
3. Add the fresh tomatoes, water, vinegar, and half of the basil.
4. Season with the salt the pepper, add the sweet paprika and hot pepper and simmer over medium-low heat for 40 minutes.
5. Transfer soup in the blender, and add 2 tablespoon olive oil.
6. Chop the remaining sun-dried tomatoes, mix them with milk and add in a blender.
7. Add remaining basil and some more olive oil. Blend until smooth and creamy.
8. Store soup in a freezer-safe container, and keep in a freezer.

Servings: 6

Preparation Time: 55 minutes

Nutrition Facts

Serving size: 1/6 of a recipe (9.9 ounces)

Percent daily values based on the Reference Daily Intake (RDI) for a 2000 calorie diet.

Nutrition information calculated from recipe ingredients.

Amount Per Serving

Calories 165,32

Calories From Fat (67%) 110,1

% Daily Value

Total Fat 12,59g 19%

Saturated Fat 2,15g 11%

Cholesterol 3,25mg 1%

Sodium 76,52mg 3%

Potassium 583,97mg 17%

Total Carbohydrates 12,03g 4%

Fiber 2,71g 11%

Sugar 5,2g

Creamy Zucchini and Potato Soup

Ingredients

1/4 cup olive oil

1 red onion, finely chopped

1 lb of zucchini cut in slices

1 lb of potatoes cut in cubes

1 cup of carrots sliced

6 cups of water

1 Tbsp of herbs seasonings

1 cup of fresh cream

Salt and ground black pepper to taste

Instructions

1. Clean zucchini, carrots, and potatoes and cut into cubes.
2. Heat the oil in a large pot and sauté the onion with little salt and pepper until soft.
3. Add zucchini, potatoes, and carrots; pour 6 cups of water.
4. Season with the salt and pepper and add the seasonings; stir well.
5. Cover and cook for about 20 - 25 minutes over medium heat.
6. Add the cream and mashed well the vegetables; cook for about 5 minutes.
7. Taste and adjust seasonings.
8. Allow cooling completely on room temperature.
9. Store in a freezer-safe container or bags and place in your freezer.

Servings: 8

Preparation Time: 35 minutes

Nutrition Facts

Serving size: 1/8 of a recipe (12.4 ounces)

Percent daily values based on the Reference Daily Intake (RDI) for a 2000 calorie diet.

Nutrition information calculated from recipe ingredients.

Amount Per Serving

Calories 258,49

Calories From Fat (70%) 179,8

% Daily Value

Total Fat 20,43g 31%

Saturated Fat 8,61g 43%

Cholesterol 40,76mg 14%

Sodium 104mg 4%

Potassium 466,31mg 13%

Total Carbohydrates 17,46g 6%

Fiber 2,39g 10%

Sugar 2,54g

Protein 3,08g 6%

Healthy Nettle Soup with Feta

Ingredients

1 1/2 lbs bunch of nettles

1 onion finely chopped

2 cloves garlic finely chopped

3 Tbsp olive oil

6 cups of water

1 cup Feta cheese crumbled

Salt and pepper to taste

Instructions

1. Cut the stems of nettles wearing gloves, and wash in water.
2. Cut nettles with the sharp knife.
3. Pour the oil to the inner stainless steel pot in the Instant Pot.
4. Add all ingredients (except Feta) in your Instant Pot.
5. Lock lid into place and set on the SOUP/STEW setting for 6 minutes.
6. When the cooking time finished using the Quick Release,
7. Transfer the soup in your blender and add crumbled Feta cheese. Blend until smooth and creamy.
8. Store soup in a freezer-safe bag, and keep in a freezer.

Servings: 6

Preparation Time: 20 minutes

Nutrition Facts

Serving size: 1/6 of a recipe (13.7 ounces)

Percent daily values based on the Reference Daily Intake (RDI) for a 2000 calorie diet.

Nutrition information calculated from recipe ingredients.

Amount Per Serving

Calories 182,94

Calories From Fat (59%) 107,85

% Daily Value

Total Fat 12,22g 19%

Saturated Fat 4,68g 23%

Cholesterol 22,25mg 7%

Sodium 388,66mg 16%

Potassium 430,47mg 12%

Total Carbohydrates 11,75g 4%

Fiber 8,19g 33%

Sugar 2,18g

Protein 6,91g 14%

Instant Broccoli Soup

Ingredients

1/4 cup olive oil

1 cup broccoli cut into a bite-sized florets

1 1/2 lbs. of zucchini sliced

1 cup fresh basil leaves, finely chopped

1 tsp fresh marjoram finely chopped

1 tsp fresh thyme finely chopped

1 tsp cumin seed, ground

4 cups water

Salt and ground pepper to taste

Instructions

1. Pour the oil in your Instant Pot and add all ingredients.
2. Lock lid into place and set on the MANUAL setting for 2 minutes.
3. When the timer beeps, press "Cancel" and carefully flip the Quick Release valve to let the pressure out.
4. Transfer the soup in a fast-speed blender, and blend until smooth.
5. Taste and adjust seasonings to taste.
6. Allow soup to cool at room temperature.
7. Store soup in freezer-safe container or bag, and keep in a freezer.

Servings: 6

Preparation Time: 10 minutes

Nutrition Facts

Serving size: 1/6 of a recipe (11 ounces)

Percent daily values based on the Reference Daily Intake (RDI) for a 2000 calorie diet.

Nutrition information calculated from recipe ingredients.

Amount Per Serving

Calories 105,37

Calories From Fat (80%) 84,08

% Daily Value

Total Fat 9,53g 15%

Saturated Fat 1,35g 7%

Cholesterol 0mg 0%

Sodium 115,04mg 5%

Potassium 364,82mg 10%

Total Carbohydrates 4,55g 2%

Fiber 1,32g 5%

Sugar 2,87g

Protein 2,02g 4%

Instant Chicken and Arugula Soup

Ingredients

2 Tbsp olive oil

1 cup chopped onion

1 1/2 lbs chicken thighs, skinless boneless

4 celery stalks, chopped

1 Tbsp dried oregano

2 cups arugula, chopped

1 tsp fennel seeds

2 quarts water

Salt and pepper to taste

Instructions

1. Cut the chicken in small cubes.
2. Wash and cut vegetables.
3. Press SAUTÉ button on your Instant Pot. Sauté the chickens, onions with a little salt about 5 minutes.
4. Add all remaining ingredients and stir well.
5. Lock lid into place and set on the SOUP/STEW on HIGH pressure for 12 minutes.
6. When the timer beeps, press "Cancel" and carefully flip the Quick Release valve to let the pressure out.
7. Taste and adjust salt and pepper to taste.
8. Pour soup in freezer-safe container or bag, and keep in a freezer.

Servings: 6

Preparation Time: 30 minutes

Nutrition Facts

Serving size: 1/6 of a recipe (11.9 ounces)

Percent daily values based on the Reference Daily Intake (RDI) for a 2000 calorie diet.

Nutrition information calculated from recipe ingredients.

Amount Per Serving

Calories 215,22

Calories From Fat (42%) 90,43

% Daily Value

Total Fat 10,15g 16%

Saturated Fat 2,1g 11%

Cholesterol 94,95mg 32%

Sodium 1752,8mg 73%

Potassium 551,3mg 16%

Total Carbohydrates 4,97g 2%

Fiber 1,38g 6%

Sugar 1,94g

Protein 25,03g 50%

Instant Sweet Potato Soup
with Coconut Milk

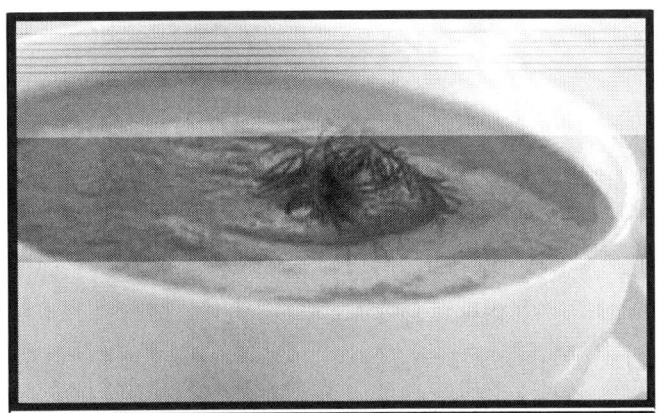

Ingredients

2 Tbsp of garlic-infused olive oil

1 Tbsp coconut oil

2 sweet potatoes, peeled

2 carrots, peeled and sliced or grated

2 cups of water

1 tsp of turmeric

1 tsp of cumin

Sea salt to taste

3/4 cup coconut milk from a can

1 Tbsp sesame seeds (optional)

Instructions

1. Clean and cut the carrots, garlic on the washers.
2. Press SAUTÉ button on your Instant Pot.
3. When the word "hot" appears on the display, add the olive and coconut oil and sauté sweet potatoes, carrots, ginger, turmeric, cumin and a pinch of salt for 5 - 6 minutes; stir frequently.
4. Pour water and the coconut milk and give a good stir.
5. Lock lid into place and set on the SOUP/STEW setting for 15 minutes.
6. Use a Natural release, and then carefully open the lid.
7. Transfer soup in a blender, add the coconut milk and blend until smooth.
8. Taste and adjust salt to taste.
9. Sprinkle with the sesame seeds and allow to cool.
10. Store soup in freezer safe bag or container and keep in a freezer.

Servings: 6

Preparation Time: 30 minutes

Nutrition Facts

Serving size: 1/6 of a recipe (11.9 ounces)

Percent daily values based on the Reference Daily Intake (RDI) for a 2000 calorie diet.

Nutrition information calculated from recipe ingredients.

Amount Per Serving

Calories 215,22

Calories From Fat (42%) 90,43

% Daily Value

Total Fat 10,15g 16%

Saturated Fat 2,1g 11%

Cholesterol 94,95mg 32%

Sodium 1752,8mg 73%

Potassium 551,3mg 16%

Total Carbohydrates 4,97g 2%

Fiber 1,38g 6%

Sugar 1,94g

Protein 25,03g 50%

Light Collard Greens Soup

Ingredients

2 Tbsp olive oil

1 onion finely chopped

2 small potatoes, cut in cubes

2 bay leaves

6 cups water

1 lb raw collard greens (stem removed and leaves cut roughly)

2 small tomatoes - peeled, seeded and chopped

1 tsp fresh rosemary

1/2 tsp fresh thyme, finely chopped

Salt and pepper to taste

Instructions

1. Heat the oil in a large pot.
2. Sauté the onion with a pinch of salt for 2 - 3 minutes,
3. Add the potato, bay leaves, and water.
4. Bring the mixture to a boil, and then reduce heat.
5. Cover and cook until potatoes are very tender, about 15 minutes.
6. Discard the bay leaves.
7. Add the collard greens, fresh rosemary, thyme, and tomatoes.
8. Cook until collard greens are wilted, about 2 - 4 minutes.
9. Adjust salt and pepper to taste; stir well.
10. Allow to cool, and then store soup in a freezer-safe container, and place in a freezer.

Servings: 8

Preparation Time: 25 minutes

Nutrition Facts

Serving size: 1/8 of a recipe (11.6 ounces)

Percent daily values based on the Reference Daily Intake (RDI) for a 2000 calorie diet.

Nutrition information calculated from recipe ingredients.

Amount Per Serving

Calories 92,22

Calories From Fat (36%) 32,99

% Daily Value

Total Fat 3,75g 6%

Saturated Fat 0,53g 3%

Cholesterol 0mg 0%

Sodium 94,34mg 4%

Potassium 380,41mg 11%

Total Carbohydrates 13,49g 4%

Fiber 3,69g 15%

Sugar 2,13g

Protein 2,73g 5%

Mediterranean Octopus Stew

Ingredients

1 octopus cleaned

2 Tbsp of vinegar

1/2 cup of white wine

4 bay leaves

1/4 cup of olive oil

2 lbs of small pearl onions

2 cloves of garlic

2 lbs of fresh tomatoes

2 cups water

1 - 2 tsp allspice

Sea salt and ground black pepper to taste

Instructions

1. Clean pearl onions and keep them whole.
2. Place the octopus pieces in a pot along with wine, vinegar and bay leaves; boil for about 25 - 30 minutes.
3. Once cooked, remove octopus from the water; discard bay leaves
4. Place the octopus in a large frying skillet along with tomatoes, oil, pearl onions, allspice, and water; season with the salt and black pepper.
5. Cook on medium heat for 15 minutes or until sauce is thickened; stir occasionally.
6. Remove from heat and allow to cool.
7. Store the stew in freezer-safe container or bag, and keep in a freezer.

Servings: 8

Preparation Time: 25 minutes

Nutrition Facts

Serving size: 1/8 of a recipe (11.6 ounces)

Percent daily values based on the Reference Daily Intake (RDI) for a 2000 calorie diet.

Nutrition information calculated from recipe ingredients.

Amount Per Serving

Calories 92,22

Calories From Fat (36%) 32,99

% Daily Value

Total Fat 3,75g 6%

Saturated Fat 0,53g 3%

Cholesterol 0mg 0%

Sodium 94,34mg 4%

Potassium 380,41mg 11%

Total Carbohydrates 13,49g 4%

Fiber 3,69g 15%

Sugar 2,13g

Protein 2,73g 5%

Pesto Chicken and Spinach Soup

Ingredients

2 Tbsp olive oil

1 carrot, cubed

1/2 red bell pepper, cut in cubes

1 chicken breast, without skin and bone, cut into quarters

1 stalk of celery

1 1/4 quart water

1 tsp garlic powder

1 1/2 tsp dry marjoram

6 oz fresh baby spinach, coarsely chopped

1/2 cup parmesan, grated

1/3 cup of fresh basil leaves

Sea salt and pepper, freshly ground

Instructions

1. Heat the olive oil in a deep pot over medium-high heat.
2. Add the carrot, pepper and chicken cubes.
3. Cook for 3-4 minutes, stirring often until browned.
4. Add the garlic powder and salt, and stir for 1 minute.
5. Add water, celery, and marjoram and bring to a boil over high heat.
6. Simmer until the chicken is done for 5 - 7 minutes.
7. Remove the chicken to a plate and allow it cool.
8. Put the spinach in the saucepan and cook for about 5 minutes.
9. In a blender put 1 tablespoon of olive oil, parmesan, and basil and beat until homogenized, adding some water if necessary.
10. Cut the chicken into bites and put it together with the pesto in the pot.
11. Cook until warm for 3 - 4 minutes.
12. Taste and adjust seasonings.
13. Allow to cool, and then store soup in a freezer-safe container, and keep in a freezer.

Servings: 6

Preparation Time: 45 minutes

Nutrition Facts

Serving size: 1/6 of a recipe (10.3 ounces)

Percent daily values based on the Reference Daily Intake (RDI) for a 2000 calorie diet.

Nutrition information calculated from recipe ingredients.

Amount Per Serving

Calories 131,75

Calories From Fat (54%) 70,59

% Daily Value

Total Fat 8,02g 12%

Saturated Fat 2,51g 13%

Cholesterol 20,93mg 7%

Sodium 177,18mg 7%

Potassium 305,11mg 9%

Total Carbohydrates 6,57g 2%

Fiber 2,88g 12%

Sugar 2,11g

Protein 9,68g 19%

Smooth Cauliflower Soup

Ingredients

1 head of cauliflower

2 leeks

3 Tbsp of olive oil

3 cloves garlic

1 hot pepper

1 Tbsp of Italian seasoning

1 Tbsp fresh parsley finely chopped

6 cups of water

Instructions

1. Heat the olive oil in a pot and sauté chopped leeks with a pinch of salt until tender.
2. Add the garlic, pepper and sauté for further 2 minutes.
3. Clean and rinse the cauliflower and cut into flowerets.
4. Place the cauliflower in a pot and pour water just enough to cover all of the vegetables.
5. Season with Italian seasonings and add the parsley
6. Cover and cook on medium heat for about 15 minutes or until cauliflower is cooked.
7. Transfer soup in a blender and blend until smooth and creamy.
8. Allow soup to cool and then store in a freezer-safe glass or plastic container.
9. Keep in the freezer for 4 months.

Servings: 6

Preparation Time: 30 minutes

Nutrition Facts

Serving size: 1/6 of a recipe (11.3 ounces)

Percent daily values based on the Reference Daily Intake (RDI) for a 2000 calorie diet.

Nutrition information calculated from recipe ingredients.

Amount Per Serving

Calories 93,1

Calories From Fat (66%) 61,91

% Daily Value

Total Fat 7,02g 11%

Saturated Fat 0,98g 5%

Cholesterol 0mg 0%

Sodium 27,31mg 1%

Potassium 199,19mg 6%

Total Carbohydrates 7,36g 2%

Fiber 1,6g 6%

Sugar 2,02g

Protein 1,47g 3%

Tomato Soup with Rice

Ingredients

4 cups of tomato juice

1/2 celery root sliced

1 cup of water

1 Tbsp fresh basil finely chopped

1/4 cup of olive oil

1 hot pepper

1 tsp of Italian seasonings

1/2 cup rice

Salt and black pepper to taste

Instructions

1. In a pot boil the celery root for about 10 minutes.
2. Add all remaining ingredients and stir well.
3. Cover and cook over medium heat for about 15 -17 minutes.
4. Taste and adjust seasonings.
5. Remove from heat and allow to cool
6. Store in a freezer-safe container; keep in the freezer for 4 months.

Servings: 6

Preparation Time: 30 minutes

Nutrition Facts

Serving size: 1/6 of a recipe (11.9 ounces)

Percent daily values based on the Reference Daily Intake (RDI) for a 2000 calorie diet.

Nutrition information calculated from recipe ingredients.

Amount Per Serving

Calories 210,26

Calories From Fat (40%) 84,14

% Daily Value

Total Fat 9,58g 15%

Saturated Fat 1,35g 7%

Cholesterol 0mg 0%

Sodium 580,52mg 24%

Potassium 713,54mg 20%

Total Carbohydrates 30,3g 10%

Fiber 4,14g 17%

Sugar 9,95g

Protein 3,4g 7%

Winter Turkey Stew

Ingredients

2 Tbsp sunflower oil

1 large onion cut into small cubes

1-1/2 lbs turkey meat, boneless and cut into 1-inch cubes

1 cup tomato peeled and cut into chunks

1 cup bell pepper finely sliced

2 clove of garlic finely chopped

2 Tbsp fresh lemon juice

1 tsp Italian seasoning

Salt and ground black pepper to taste

Instructions

1. Heat the oil in a large pot and sauté the onion and turkey meat for about 3 - 4 minutes.
2. Add all remaining ingredients, cover, reduce heat to low and simmer about 15 minutes.
3. Stew is ready when turkey meat is soft.
4. Store your stew in a freezer-safe container and keep in a freezer for a couple of months.

Servings: 4

Preparation Time: 25 minutes

Nutrition Facts

Serving size: 1/4 of a recipe (10.6 ounces)

Percent daily values based on the Reference Daily Intake (RDI) for a 2000 calorie diet.

Nutrition information calculated from recipe ingredients.

Amount Per Serving

Calories 306,87

Calories From Fat (44%) 136,13

% Daily Value

Total Fat 15,27g 23%

Saturated Fat 3,26g 16%

Cholesterol 122,47mg 41%

Sodium 2045,3mg 85%

Potassium 718,54mg 21%

Total Carbohydrates 11g 4%

Fiber 2,14g 9%

Sugar 6,01g

Protein 30,96g 62%

FINGER FOOD/
SNACKS

◆ ◆ ◆

Baked Zucchini Patties

Ingredients

4 organics eggs

2 lbs of zucchini

1 1/2 cups of grated Parmesan

1 cup of sour cream

1 1/4 cups of olive oil

1 cup of semolina

1/4 cup of wheat flour

1 Tbsp fresh parsley chopped

1 Tbsp of baking powder

Instructions

1. Preheat oven to 360 F/180C.
2. Line a baking pan with parchment paper; set aside.
3. Clean zucchini; grate them and place in a colander to drain.
4. In a meanwhile, beat eggs with all remaining ingredients until a compact mixture is achieved.
5. Shape patties and place onto prepared baking pan.
6. Place in oven and bake for 30 minutes.
7. Remove for oven and allow to cool.
8. Place in a freezer safe container and keep in freezer up to two months.

Servings: 10

Preparation Time: 40 minutes

Nutrition Facts

Serving size: 1/10 of a recipe (7.2 ounces)

Percent daily values based on the Reference Daily Intake (RDI) for a 2000 calorie diet.

Nutrition information calculated from recipe ingredients.

Amount Per Serving

Calories 416,28

Calories From Fat (70%) 289,77

% Daily Value

Total Fat 32,83g 51%

Saturated Fat 8,96g 45%

Cholesterol 99,56mg 33%

Sodium 430,42mg 18%

Potassium 351,16mg 10%

Total Carbohydrates 19,17g 6%

Fiber 1,65g 7%

Sugar 3,29g

Protein 12,3g 25%

Delicious Butter Bannock

Ingredients

1 cup of Greek yogurt

1 tsp of baking soda

1 cup of fresh butter

1 tsp of salt

2 cups of flour

1 cup of grated cheese, any

Instructions

1. Preheat oven to 350F/175 C.
2. Oil a baking pan with the butter; set aside.
3. Combine Greek yogurt and baking soda in a mixing bowl.
4. Add all remaining ingredients and beat with the help of an electric mixer.
5. Beat until getting the hard dough.

6. Transfer dough on a working surface and roll with the rolling pin.
7. Cut dough in round pieces with the toothed knife and place in a prepared pan.
8. Bake for 35 - 40 minutes.
9. Remove from oven and allow to cool.
10. Wrap every bannock in wax paper and place in a plastic freezer bags. Keep in the freezer for 6 months.

Servings: 8

Preparation Time: 55 minutes

Nutrition Facts

Serving size: 1/8 of a recipe (4 ounces)

Percent daily values based on the Reference Daily Intake (RDI) for a 2000 calorie diet.

Nutrition information calculated from recipe ingredients.

Amount Per Serving

Calories 371,07

Calories From Fat (64%) 236,32

% Daily Value

Total Fat 26,9g 41%

Saturated Fat 16,79g 84%

Cholesterol 72,01mg 24%

Sodium 642,88mg 27%

Potassium 55,93mg 2%

Total Carbohydrates 24,37g 8%

Fiber 0,84g 3%

Sugar 0,21g

Protein 8,28g 17%

Instant Asparagus Sticks

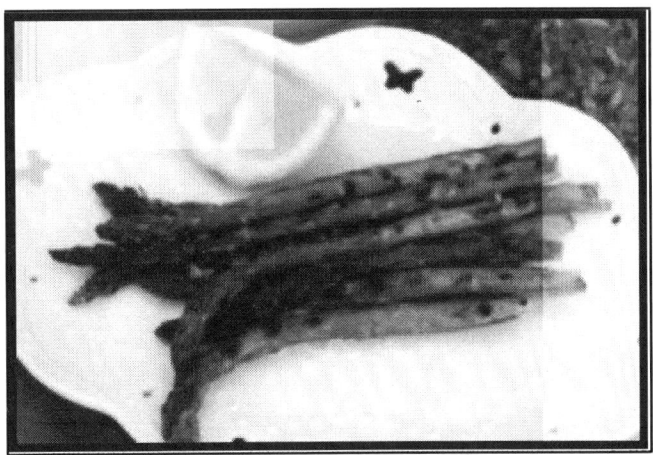

Ingredients

1 lb asparagus - cleaned

1 cup water

1 Tbsp onion powder

1 tsp of garlic powder

2 Tbsp garlic-infused olive oil

Sea salt and freshly ground pepper

Instructions

1. With a sharp knife, clean asparagus. Cut asparagus into equal lengths pieces.
2. Place the steamer basket into the Instant Pot and pour

the water.
3. Place the asparagus onto the steamer basket.
4. Sprinkle the asparagus with olive oil, garlic and onion powder.
5. Lock lid into place and set on the STEAMING setting for 3 minutes.
6. When the timer beeps, press "Cancel" and flip the Quick Release valve.
7. Open the lid and adjust salt and pepper.
8. Freeze asparagus in a heavy-duty freezer bags.

Servings: 4

Preparation Time: 15 minutes

Nutrition Facts

Serving size: 1/4 of a recipe (5.2 ounces)

Percent daily values based on the Reference Daily Intake (RDI) for a 2000 calorie diet.

Nutrition information calculated from recipe ingredients.

Amount Per Serving

Calories 81,52

Calories From Fat (74%) 60,53

% Daily Value

Total Fat 6,85g 11%

Saturated Fat 0,96g 5%

Cholesterol 0mg 0%

Sodium 4,98mg <1%

Potassium 162,24mg 5%

Total Carbohydrates 4,53g 2%

Fiber 1,74g 7%

Sugar 1,39g

Protein 1,78g 4%

Keto Parmesan Triangles

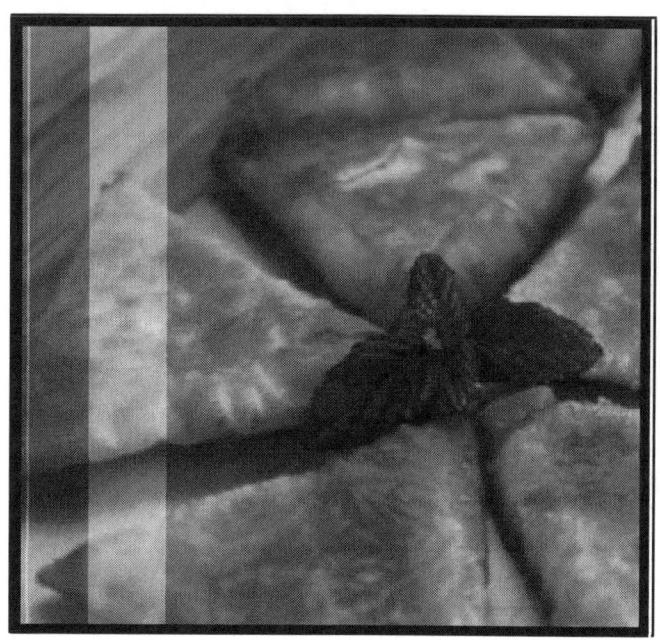

Ingredients

1/2 cup almond flour

1 Tbsp almond butter (unsweetened)

1 1/4 cup parmesan cheese

1/4 tsp rosemary, finely chopped

1/4 tsp fresh basil, finely chopped

1/4 tsp fresh oregano, finely chopped

1 large egg

Instructions

1. Preheat the oven to 350 F/175C. Line a baking sheet with parchment paper.
2. In a bowl, combine the almond flour, almond butter, and grated parmesan cheese.
3. Add fresh and chopped basil, rosemary and oregano; give a good stir.
4. Add the egg and stir again.
5. Scoop a teaspoon of the mixture onto a prepared baking sheet. Bake for 15 minutes or until golden brown.
6. Remove from the oven and allow to cool completely.
7. Wrap triangles in a wax pepper and place in a freezer safe plastic bag.
8. Keep in freezer up to 2 months.

Servings: 6

Preparation Time: 25 minutes

Nutrition Facts

Serving size: 1/6 of a recipe   (2 ounces)

Percent daily values based on the Reference Daily Intake (RDI) for a 2000 calorie diet.

Nutrition information calculated from recipe ingredients.

Amount Per Serving

Calories 136,38

Calories From Fat (60%) 82,4

% Daily Value

Total Fat 9,43g 15%

Saturated Fat 4,7g 24%

Cholesterol 53mg 18%

Sodium 394,34mg 16%

Potassium 65,21mg 2%

Total Carbohydrates 1,65g <1%

Fiber 0,33g 1%

Sugar 0,38g

Protein 11,24g 22%

Raspberry Muffins (Gluten-free; Sugar-free)

Ingredients

2 1/2 cups gluten-free flour (buckwheat, millet)

2 tsp baking powder

2 tsp cinnamon

2 pastured or organic eggs

1/4 cup stevia sweetener granulated

1/4 cup coconut milk

2 Tbsp Extra-virgin olive oil

3 Tbsp lemon juice (freshly squeezed)

1 cup raspberries, chopped (fresh or frozen)

Instructions

1. Preheat the oven to 360 F/180 C.
2. Grease a muffin tin with little oil; set aside.
3. Combine the gluten-free flour, baking powder, and cinnamon; set aside.
4. In a separate bowl, mix all remaining ingredients. Combine the flour mixture to the eggs mixture; stir well.
5. Pour the batter in 12 muffin cups.
6. Bake about 30 minutes or until golden brown.
7. Remove muffins from oven and allow to cool.
8. Wrap muffins with foil and place in freezer safe bags. Keep in freezer up to 2 - 3 months.

Servings: 12

Preparation Time: 35 minutes

Nutrition Facts

Serving size: 1/12 of a recipe (2.4 ounces)

Percent daily values based on the Reference Daily Intake (RDI) for a 2000 calorie diet.

Nutrition information calculated from recipe ingredients.

Amount Per Serving

Calories 132,19

Calories From Fat (32%) 42,15

% Daily Value

Total Fat 4,88g 8%

Saturated Fat 1,67g 8%

Cholesterol 31mg 10%

Sodium 96,76mg 4%

Potassium 181,11mg 5%

Total Carbohydrates 20,14g 7%

Fiber 3,16g 13%

Sugar 1,16g

Protein 4,35g 9%

Savory Sesame Sticks

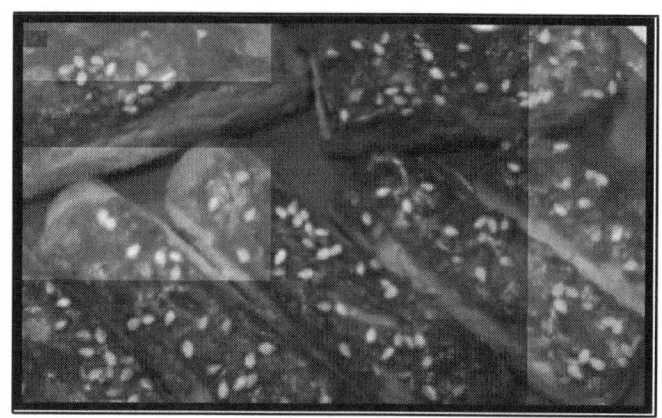

Ingredients

1 lb of wheat flour

1 tsp of salt

1 1/4 cups of fresh butter

3/4 cup of milk

2 Tbsp of fresh yeast

2 tsp of sugar

2 free-range eggs

Coating

1 egg yolk, beaten

1/4 cup of sesame seeds

Instructions

1. Preheat oven to 360 F/180 C.
2. Heat the milk with sugar and yeast, and let it foam.
3. Combine milk/yeast mixture with remaining ingredients and beat with an electric mixer until soft dough is achieved.
4. Roll dough with the rolling pin to the 0.4-inch thickness. With the sharp knife cut the dough in square or rectangle shape.
5. Place the sticks in a baking pan and brush with beaten yolk; sprinkle generously with sesame seeds.
6. Bake for 15 minutes or until getting a nice golden brown color.
7. Allow cooling completely.
8. Wrap each sesame stick in wax paper and place in an airtight container; keep in a freezer.

Servings: 10

Preparation Time: 30 minutes

Nutrition Facts

Serving size: 1/10 of a recipe (4 ounces)

Percent daily values based on the Reference Daily Intake (RDI) for a 2000 calorie diet.

Nutrition information calculated from recipe ingredients.

Amount Per Serving

Calories 442,79

Calories From Fat (56%) 248,35

% Daily Value

Total Fat 28,38g 44%

Saturated Fat 15,79g 79%

Cholesterol 117,68mg 39%

Sodium 262,07mg 11%

Potassium 147,64mg 4%

Total Carbohydrates 38,88g 13%

Fiber 2,58g 10%

Sugar 1,97g

Protein 9,08g 18%

Zucchini "Ducats" with Parmesan and Herbs

Ingredients

6 zucchini, halved

1 cup Parmesan cheese, shredded

1/4 tsp dried parsley

1/2 tsp dried thyme

1/4 tsp tarragon (chopped)

1/4 tsp sage leaves chopped

1/2 tsp Salt and freshly ground black pepper

Instructions

1. Preheat oven to 350 degrees F/175C.

2. Place zucchini halves on 2 baking sheets lined with parchment paper.
3. Combine the Parmesan cheese, parsley, thyme, sage, tarragon, and the salt and black pepper.
4. Sprinkle each zucchini slice with cheese-herb mixture evenly. Bake for 15 - 17 minutes.
5. Place zucchini in resealable plastic bags and keep refrigerated up to 4 days.

Servings: 8

Preparation Time: 25 minutes

Nutrition Facts

Serving size: 1/8 of a recipe (5,9 ounces).

Percent daily values based on the Reference Daily Intake (RDI) for a 2000 calorie diet.

Nutrition information calculated from recipe ingredients.

Amount Per Serving

Calories 81,48

Calories From Fat (44%) 35,87

% Daily Value

Total Fat 4,1g 6%

Saturated Fat 2,3g 12%

Cholesterol 11mg 4%

Sodium 203,73mg 8%

Potassium 425,42mg 12%

Total Carbohydrates 5,62g 2%

Fiber 1,69g 7%

Sugar 3,99g

Protein 6,73g 13%

SAUCES/DRESSING

◆ ◆ ◆

Delicious Parsley Dip

Ingredients

1 cup parsley finely chopped

1/2 cup breadcrumbs

1 onion finely chopped

1/2 cup garlic-infused olive oil

Lemon juice from 1 lemon, freshly squeezed

Salt and ground pepper to taste

Instructions

1. Wash the parsley, cut it into small pieces.
2. Add parsley in your blender along with the bread crumbs, olive oil, chopped onion, and salt and pepper;

blend until smooth.
3. Taste and adjust salt and pepper.
4. Keep in a covered container for 5 to 6 days.

Servings: 3

Preparation Time: 10 minutes

Nutrition Facts

Serving size: 1/3 of a recipe (4 ounces)

Percent daily values based on the Reference Daily Intake (RDI) for a 2000 calorie diet.

Nutrition information calculated from recipe ingredients.

Amount Per Serving

Calories 405,94

Calories From Fat (81%) 328,44

% Daily Value

Total Fat 37,17g 57%

Saturated Fat 5,23g 26%

Cholesterol 0mg 0%

Sodium 338,17mg 14%

Potassium 185,27mg 5%

Total Carbohydrates 16,77g 6%

Fiber 1,74g 7%

Sugar 2,32g

Protein 3,21g 6%

Skordalia - Crushed Garlic Sauce

Ingredients

4 slices of old bread, only crumbs soaked and well drained

3 boiled potatoes

4 cloves garlic

Salt to taste

1 cup corn oil

3 Tbsp vinegar

Instructions

1. Soak bread; cover and set aside.
2. Clean and boil the potatoes for 15 to 20 minutes; drain.

3. Place the potatoes in a blender along with drained bread, garlic, salt, corn oil, and vinegar.
4. Blend until all ingredients are combined well.
5. Taste and adjust salt.
6. Skordalia sauce can be served with fish, fried or boiled vegetables.
7. Keep in a glass jar for one week in a refrigerator.

Servings: 6

Preparation Time: 30 minutes

Nutrition Facts

Serving size: 1/6 of a recipe (5 ounces)

Percent daily values based on the Reference Daily Intake (RDI) for a 2000 calorie diet.

Nutrition information calculated from recipe ingredients.

Amount Per Serving

Calories 280,12

Calories From Fat (59%) 166,47

% Daily Value

Total Fat 18,84g 29%

Saturated Fat 2,5g 13%

Cholesterol 0mg 0%

Sodium 139,55mg 6%

Potassium 419,52mg 12%

Total Carbohydrates 25,61g 9%

Fiber 2,47g 10%

Sugar 1,46g

Protein 3,26g 7%

Homemade Basil Sauce
with Pine Nuts

Ingredients

5 cups of fresh basil finely chopped

5 cloves garlic minced

3/4 cup pine nuts

1/2 cup hard yellow cheese, ground

1/2 cup parmesan cheese

1 cup extra-virgin olive oil

Black pepper to taste

Pinch of salt

Instructions

1. Place all ingredients in your high-fast blender, and blend until smooth and thick.
2. We can keep a sauce refrigerate in a sealed glass jar for several weeks.
3. This sauce is an ideal sauce for all kinds of pasta.

Servings: 6

Preparation Time: 10 minutes

Nutrition Facts

Serving size: 1/6 of a recipe (4.1 ounces)

Percent daily values based on the Reference Daily Intake (RDI) for a 2000 calorie diet.

Nutrition information calculated from recipe ingredients.

Amount Per Serving

Calories 161,67

Calories From Fat (74%) 119,58

% Daily Value

Total Fat 14,16g 22%

Saturated Fat 2,29g 11%

Cholesterol 7,33mg 2%

Sodium 178,07mg 7%

Potassium 227,2mg 6%

Total Carbohydrates 4,39g 1%

Fiber 1,28g 5%

Sugar 0,81g

Protein 6,8g 14%

Homemade Roquefort Sauce

Ingredients

7 oz blue cheese

2 1/2 cups cream

2 Tbsp fresh parsley chopped

Black pepper to taste

Instructions

1. Mash the blue cheese with a fork and put it in a saucepan.
2. Add the cream, parsley, and pepper.
3. Bring to boil over medium heat for about 4-5 minutes or until the sauce is thick.
4. Let it cool at room temperature.
5. Store in a glass container and keep refrigerated for 4 days or store in a freezer-safe bag, and keep in a freezer.

Servings: 6

Preparation Time: 15 minutes

Nutrition Facts

Serving size: 1/6 of a recipe (3.2 ounces)

Percent daily values based on the Reference Daily Intake (RDI) for a 2000 calorie diet.

Nutrition information calculated from recipe ingredients.

Amount Per Serving

Calories 289,66

Calories From Fat (85%) 245,74

% Daily Value

Total Fat 27,95g 43%

Saturated Fat 17,65g 88%

Cholesterol 93,02mg 31%

Sodium 481,08mg 20%

Potassium 132,58mg 4%

Total Carbohydrates 2,41g < 1%

Fiber 0,11g < 1%

Edward Cruz

Sugar 0,23g

Protein 8,16g 16%

Hot Tropical Sauce

Ingredients

2 Tbsp olive oil

2 Tbsp of butter

1 onion finely chopped

4 green onions finely chopped

3 cloves garlic minced

1 1/2 Tbsp hot curry sauce powder

1/2 green apple, peeled and finely sliced

1/2 pineapple

1 banana

1 Tbsp coconut milk

1/2 cup of water

Salt and ground white pepper to taste

1 Tbsp balsamic vinegar (optional)

1 Tbsp honey (optional)

1/2 Tbsp fresh lemon juice (optional)

Instructions

1. Pour the olive oil, butter in a frying skillet over medium-high heat.
2. When hot, sauté the onion, green onions, garlic with salt and pepper for 3 - 4 minutes; stir.
3. Pour hot curry sauce and stir for further one minute.
4. Pour the sauce in your high-speed blender along with remaining ingredients from the list above; blend until a thick and creamy sauce is achieved.
5. Pour in a container, cover and refrigerate up to 4 days or store a sauce in a freezer-safe container, and keep in a freezer.

Servings: 8

Preparation Time: 15 minutes

Nutrition Facts

Serving size: 1/8 of a recipe (5.3 ounces)

Percent daily values based on the Reference Daily Intake (RDI) for a 2000 calorie diet.

Nutrition information calculated from recipe ingredients.

Amount Per Serving

Calories 144,12

Calories From Fat (45%) 64,75

% Daily Value

Total Fat 7,36g 11%

Saturated Fat 2,88g 14%

Cholesterol 9,84mg 3%

Sodium 126,32mg 5%

Potassium 173,98mg 5%

Total Carbohydrates 19,64g 7%

Fiber 1,97g 8%

Sugar 10,84g

Edward Cruz

Protein 1,72g 3%

Mushroom Sauce (for Roasted Meat)

Ingredients

1 1/4 lbs mushrooms chopped and drained

3 onions finely chopped

1 1/4 cups cream

3 Tbsp fresh butter

Salt and ground black pepper

Instructions

1. Heat the butter in a large frying skillet over medium-strong heat.
2. Add the onion and a pinch of salt and sauté for about 3 minutes; stir.
3. Add the mushrooms, reduce heat and cook on low heat for 10 minutes.

4. Finally, add the cream, salt, pepper, and simmer sauce until thick.
5. Remove from heat, and let it cool at room temperature
6. Pour your sauce in a container with a lid, and refrigerate for up to 4 to 5 days.
7. Also, you can freeze this sauce in a resealable freezer bag.
8. To defrost: keep in refrigerate for 12 hours. Reheat in your microwave oven. Serve with your favorite meat.

Servings: 8

Preparation Time: 20 minutes

Nutrition Facts

Serving size: 1/8 of a recipe (5 ounces)

Percent daily values based on the Reference Daily Intake (RDI) for a 2000 calorie diet.

Nutrition information calculated from recipe ingredients.

Amount Per Serving

Calories 136,53

Calories From Fat (74%) 101,12

% Daily Value

Total Fat 11,51g 18%

Saturated Fat 7,09g 35%

Cholesterol 37,03mg 12%

Sodium 13,06mg <1%

Potassium 307,6mg 9%

Total Carbohydrates 7,12g 2%

Fiber 1,49g 6%

Sugar 3,37g

Protein 3,12g 6%

CASSEROLES

◆ ◆ ◆

Absolute Summer Vege-
table Casseroles

Ingredients

2/3 cup of olive oil

3 cloves of garlic

1 large onion finely chopped

1 cup of okra

1 cup of green beans (fresh or chilled)

2 medium eggplants (cut into large pieces)

2 large zucchini (cut into large pieces)

1 bell pepper (cut into large pieces)

3 medium tomatoes grated

1 Tbsp tomato paste

1 cup of water

1 bunch of parsley (finely chopped)

1 Tbsp dried basil

1 tsp sugar

Salt and freshly ground pepper

Instructions

1. Rinse, clean and cut your vegetables.
2. Preheat the oven to 350 F/170C.
3. Heat the oil in a large pot over high heat.
4. When hot, reduce the heat and sauté onion and garlic with the salt; stir.
5. Add all remaining ingredients and sauté, stirring occasionally, for about 4 to 5 minutes.
6. Pour the mixture in an oiled casserole dish and place in your oven.
7. Bake for 15 -20 minutes.
8. Remove from the oven and let cool on room temperature.
9. Store in container with a lid, and keep refrigerated for 3 - 4 days or store in a freezer safe bags and freeze for 2 months.

Servings: 6

Preparation Time: 40 minutes

Nutrition Facts

Serving size: 1/6 of a recipe (10.8 ounces)

Percent daily values based on the Reference Daily Intake (RDI) for a 2000 calorie diet.

Nutrition information calculated from recipe ingredients.

Amount Per Serving

Calories 270,92

Calories From Fat (80%) 216,8

% Daily Value

Total Fat 24,54g 38%

Saturated Fat 3,44g 17%

Cholesterol 0mg 0%

Sodium 36,07mg 2%

Potassium 553,56mg 16%

Total Carbohydrates 12,53g 4%

Fiber 3,8g 15%

Sugar 6,83g

Protein 2,91g 6%

Artichoke Hearts with Peas and Potato Casserole

Ingredients

1/4 cup of olive oil

2 medium onions, coarsely chopped

12 -14 artichoke hearts, drained

1 1/2 cups of frozen peas

2 medium potatoes, cleaned and cut into small pieces

3 whole canned tomatoes mashed

1 Tbsp Italian seasonings

1/2 Tbsp dry rosemary, crumbly (optional)

1/2 tsp dry marjoram (or thyme)

Salt, freshly ground pepper to taste

Instructions

1. Preheat your oven to 350 F/175 C.
2. Heat the oil in a large pot and sauté the onion with a little salt for 3 - 4 minutes.
3. Add artichokes and peas and stir for 2 - 3 minutes.
4. Add potatoes, season with the Italian seasonings, rosemary, and marjoram; stir well.
5. Pour the artichoke hearts mixture in the 9x13-inch casserole dish.
6. Bake in the oven for 25 - 35 minutes.
7. Remove from the oven and let cool.
8. Keep refrigerated in a covered container for 3 - 4 days or store in an airtight freezer bag or container and place in your freezer for about 3 months.

Servings: 6

Preparation Time: 45 minutes

Nutrition Facts

Serving size: 1/6 of a recipe (13.6 ounces)

Percent daily values based on the Reference Daily Intake (RDI) for a 2000 calorie diet.

Nutrition information calculated from recipe ingredients.

Amount Per Serving

Calories 308,93

Calories From Fat (29%) 88,8

% Daily Value

Total Fat 10,13g 16%

Saturated Fat 1,36g 7%

Cholesterol 0mg 0%

Sodium 424,87mg 18%

Potassium 1117,69mg 32%

Total Carbohydrates 49,28g 16%

Fiber 14,27g 57%

Sugar 3,66g

Protein 10,93g 22%

Bacon - Pork and Vegetables Casserole

Ingredients

2 Tbsp of olive oil

1/2 lb of bacon, finely chopped

1 onion finely chopped

3 cloves of garlic

2 cups of white wine

Salt and pepper to taste

1/2 lb pork loin cut large cubes

2 cups carrots cut in rings

1 lb of potatoes

3 bay leaves

Instructions

1. Preheat oven to 350 degrees F/170 C.
2. In a deep and heavy frying skillet, heat the olive oil on medium heat.
3. Fry the bacon for 3 - 4 minutes.
4. Add the onion and garlic and sauté for 2 - 3 minutes; stir.
5. Add the pork meat and season with salt and pepper.
6. Cook, stirring occasionally, for 2 - 3 minutes.
7. Add all remaining ingredients from the list above and give a good stir.
8. Cook for 2 - 3 minutes, and then transfer the mixture in the 9x13-inch casserole pan.
9. Place in oven and bake for 50 - 60 minutes.
10. Allow to cool, and then store in a freezer airtight container.
11. Keep in freezer for 3 - 4 months.

Servings: 6

Preparation Time: 1 hour and 25 minutes

Nutrition Facts

Serving size: 1/6 of a recipe (10,5 ounces).

Percent daily values based on the Reference Daily Intake (RDI) for a 2000 calorie diet.

Nutrition information calculated from recipe ingredients.

Amount Per Serving

Calories 405,18

Calories From Fat (50%) 200,85

% Daily Value

Total Fat 22,38g 34%

Saturated Fat 6,58g 33%

Cholesterol 49,68mg 17%

Sodium 457,5mg 19%

Potassium 768,77mg 22%

Total Carbohydrates 22,03g 7%

Fiber 3,25g 13%

Sugar 4,25g

Protein 14,99g 30%

Beef and Orzo Giouvetsi Casseroles

Ingredients

1 1/2 lb beef boneless and cut in cubes

1/2 cup olive oil

1 onion finely chopped

2 cloves of garlic

1 cup of white wine

1 cup of water

3 large ripe tomatoes peeled and grated

2 Tbsp tomato paste

1/4 tsp pinch of cinnamon

Salt and ground black pepper

1/2 lb of orzo

Instructions

1. Heat the oven to 400F/200C.
2. Heat the oil in a large frying skillet over high heat.
3. Sauté the onion, garlic and beef cubes with the salt and pepper.
4. Add grated tomatoes and tomato paste; stir.
5. Pour water and wine and stir well; cook for further 2 minutes.
6. Season with the salt and pepper and add the cinnamon.
7. In a separate pot, cook the orzo in salted water for about 5 - 7 minutes.
8. Rinse over cold water and drain.
9. Transfer the beef mixture in a 9x13-inch rectangular casserole dish.
10. Add the barley and give a good stir.
11. Place a casserole dish in the oven and bake for about 20 minutes.
12. Remove from oven and allow it to cool completely.
13. Store in an airtight and freezer safe container and place in a freezer.

Servings: 6

Preparation Time: 45 minutes

Nutrition Facts

Serving size: 1/6 of a recipe (10 ounces)

Percent daily values based on the Reference Daily Intake (RDI) for a 2000 calorie diet.

Nutrition information calculated from recipe ingredients.

Amount Per Serving

Calories 531,09

Calories From Fat (58%) 339,04

% Daily Value

Total Fat 37,47g 58%

Saturated Fat 10,13g 51%

Cholesterol 68,04mg 23%

Sodium 114,9mg 5%

Potassium 568,63mg 16%

Total Carbohydrates 31,9g 11%

Fiber 2,26g 9%

Sugar 3,7g

Protein 21,46g 43%

Mediterranean Feta and Vegetable Casserole

Ingredients

0.8 lb feta cheese

0.8 lb cherry tomato, halved

1 large red pepper cut in slices

1 cup black olives, pitted and halved

2 tsp of dried oregano

Salt and ground pepper

1/4 cup garlic-infused olive oil

2 Tbsp Fresh parsley finely chopped

Instructions

1. Heat the oven to 400 °F/ 200 ° C.
2. Grease with the oil a rectangular casserole dish.
3. Cut Feta cheese in several pieces and place in casserole dish.
4. Combine halved cherry tomatoes, olives, red bell pepper in a bowl.
5. Season with the salt and pepper, and add oregano, parsley, and olive oil: toss to combine well.
6. Add the tomato mixture in a casserole dish.
7. Bake for 20 - 25 minutes.
8. Remove from the oven and let it cool completely.
9. Store in a container, cover and keep refrigerated for 3 - 4 days.

Servings: 6

Preparation Time: 35 minutes

Nutrition Facts

Serving size: 1/6 of a recipe (6.7 ounces)

Percent daily values based on the Reference Daily Intake (RDI) for a 2000 calorie diet.

Nutrition information calculated from recipe ingredients.

Amount Per Serving

Calories 285,79

Calories From Fat (75%) 215

% Daily Value

Total Fat 24,47g 38%

Saturated Fat 10,6g 53%

Cholesterol 53,83mg 18%

Sodium 876,9mg 37%

Potassium 225,98mg 6%

Total Carbohydrates 8,26g 3%

Fiber 2,06g 8%

Sugar 3,52g

Protein 9,52g 19%

Pork with Mustard and Horse-radish Casserole

Ingredients

1/4 cup of olive oil

2 lbs of pork loin, cut into large cubes

2 lbs of potatoes, peeled and cut in half

1 onion finely chopped

4 cloves of garlic

1 cup of red wine

1 Tbsp of yellow mustard

1 Tbsp of fresh horseradish grated

1 Tbsp oregano

Salt and ground pepper to taste

Instructions

1. Preheat your oven to 400 F/ 240 degrees C.
2. Heat the oil in a pot and cook the pork along with the onion and garlic.
3. Add all remaining ingredients and give a good stir.
4. Season the salt and pepper and cook for 5 minutes.
5. Transfer the mixture in the large rectangular casserole pan.
6. Bake for 40 - 45 minutes.
7. Remove from the oven and allow it to cool.
8. Store in an airtight container and keep in the freezer for 3 months.

Servings: 6

Preparation Time: 50 minutes

Nutrition Facts

Serving size: 1/6 of a recipe (12.3 ounces)

Percent daily values based on the Reference Daily Intake (RDI) for a 2000 calorie diet.

Nutrition information calculated from recipe ingredients.

Amount Per Serving

Calories 412,56

Calories From Fat (31%) 129,07

% Daily Value

Total Fat 14,5g 22%

Saturated Fat 3,14g 16%

Cholesterol 99,79mg 33%

Sodium 221,12mg 9%

Potassium 1290,91mg 37%

Total Carbohydrates 30,19g 10%

Fiber 4,18g 17%

Sugar 2,35g

Protein 37,51g 75%

Spicy Spanish Rice Casserole

Ingredients

2 Tbsp chicken fat

1 large onion finely chopped

2 cloves garlic, smashed

2 1/4 cups brown rice (or white)

3 3/4 cups chicken broth (or vegetable)

1 can (15 oz) fire-roasted tomatoes

1 tsp chili powder

1 tsp cumin

Salt and pepper to taste

Instructions

1. Preheat oven to 350 degrees F/170 C.
2. Heat the chicken fat in a large frying skillet (over medium-high heat) and sauté onion and garlic with a pinch of salt.
3. Add all remaining ingredients and give a good stir; cook for 2 - 3 minutes.
4. Transfer the rice mixture in the oiled 9x13-inch casserole pan.
5. Bake for 35 - 45 minutes or until all liquids are absorbed.
6. Allow to cool and store in an airtight container with a lid.
7. Keep refrigerated for 4 to 5 days.
8. If you want to store a meal for a longer time, store in a freezer-safe container or and keep in a freezer.

Servings: 6

Preparation Time: 55 minutes

Nutrition Facts

Serving size: 1/6 of a recipe (11.7 ounces)

Percent daily values based on the Reference Daily Intake (RDI) for a 2000 calorie diet.

Nutrition information calculated from recipe ingredients.

Amount Per Serving

Calories 340,98

Calories From Fat (20%) 67,27

% Daily Value

Total Fat 7,62g 12%

Saturated Fat 1,55g 8%

Cholesterol 3,63mg 1%

Sodium 575,89mg 24%

Potassium 315,91mg 9%

Total Carbohydrates 65,88g 22%

Fiber 5,8g 23%

Sugar 3,14g

Protein 8,47g 17%

SWEETS/DESSERTS

◆ ◆ ◆

Cognac - Chocolate Roll

Ingredients

1 1/2 cups fresh butter

1 cup of powdered sugar

1/4 cup Cognac

4 Tbsp cocoa powder

1/2 lb biscuits, plain crushed

1/2 cup of walnuts finely chopped

Instructions

1. Melt the butter in a microwave oven.
2. In a saucepan, melt butter along with powdered sugar, cocoa powder, and cognac and stir well.
3. Add crushed biscuits and walnuts and stir well.
4. Allow the mixture to cool for 10 minutes.
5. Spread the mixture onto foil or non-stick parchment

paper and wrap it in a round shape.
6. Refrigerate for 3 – 4 hours.
7. Remove from fridge and slice.
8. Freeze in a freezer-safe container for two months.

Servings: 10

Preparation Time: 20 minutes

Inactive Time: 4 hours

Nutrition Facts

Serving size: 1/10 of a recipe (3 ounces)

Percent daily values based on the Reference Daily Intake (RDI) for a 2000 calorie diet.

Nutrition information calculated from recipe ingredients.

Amount Per Serving

Calories 463,4

Calories From Fat (66%) 307,96

% Daily Value

Total Fat 35,22g 54%

Saturated Fat 18,92g 95%

Cholesterol 73,66mg 25%

Sodium 234,04mg 10%

Potassium 104,27mg 3%

Total Carbohydrates 36,43g 12%

Fiber 1,59g 6%

Sugar 22,81g

Protein 3,42g 7%

Cranberries and Hazelnuts Muffins

Ingredients

1/2 cup dried cranberries

1 cup boiling water

1 1/2 cup flour

1 Tbsp baking powder

5.50 oz brown sugar

2.50 chopped hazelnuts

2 tsp dry ginger

1 tsp cinnamon powder

1/2 tsp nutmeg

3/4 cup sour milk

3/4 cup sunflower oil

1 large free-range egg, beaten

Coating:

2 Tbsp chopped hazelnuts

1 Tbsp brown sugar

Instructions

1. Put cranberries in a bowl and add the boiling water.
2. Leave for 5-10 minutes and drain.
3. Preheat the oven to 400 F/200 C.
4. Prepare and grease 16 baking muffin cups.
5. Mix the flour with baking powder, sugar, hazelnuts, ginger, cinnamon and nutmeg in a bowl.
6. In a separate bowl, beat the egg with sunflower oil and sour milk.
7. Combine the liquid mixture to the flour mixture
8. Add the cranberries and stir well until all ingredients are combined well.
9. Pour the mixture into prepared muffin cups.
10. Sprinkle with hazelnuts and sugar and bake for about 20 minutes.
11. Remove muffins from the oven, and let cool on room temperature.
12. Keep your muffins in sealed plastic bags up to 3 days.
13. Also, you can wrap muffins in freezer bags, and freeze for

up to 2 - 3 months.

Servings: 16

Preparation Time: 40 minutes

Nutrition Facts

Serving size: 1/16 of a recipe (3 ounces)

Percent daily values based on the Reference Daily Intake (RDI) for a 2000 calorie diet.

Nutrition information calculated from recipe ingredients.

Amount Per Serving

Calories 252,95

Calories From Fat (40%) 102,37

% Daily Value

Total Fat 11,61g 18%

Saturated Fat 1,16g 6%

Cholesterol 12,08mg 4%

Sodium 112,31mg 5%

Potassium 65,92mg 2%

Total Carbohydrates 35,72g 12%

Fiber 1,71g 7%

Sugar 10,95g

Protein 2,14g 4%

Dark Knight Cake

Ingredients

1/4 cup cocoa powder unsweetened

2 cups flour, white, all-purpose

1/8 tsp salt

1/8 tsp baking powder

1/2 cup fresh butter, unsalted and melted

2 Tbsp full-fat milk

1 1/2 tsp almond extract

2 tsp vanilla extract

1/4 cup brown sugar

Instructions

1. Preheat oven to 340F/165 degrees.
2. Grease a baking dish with a little butter.
3. In a bowl, stir the cocoa powder, flour, salt and baking powder in a bowl.
4. In a separate bowl, whisk together melted butter, milk, almond and vanilla extract, and brown sugar until combined well.
5. Combine the flour mixture with the milk mixture and give a good stir.
6. Pour the batter in the prepared baking dish, and bake for 25 - 30 minutes.
7. Once ready, let cool on room temperature.
8. Place in a container and keep refrigerated up to one week.

Servings: 8

Preparation Time: 25 minutes

Nutrition Facts

Serving size: 1/8 of a recipe (2.3 ounces)

Percent daily values based on the Reference Daily Intake (RDI) for a 2000 calorie diet.

Nutrition information calculated from recipe ingredients.

Amount Per Serving

Calories 253,83

Calories From Fat (43%) 108,68

% Daily Value

Total Fat 12,27g 19%

Saturated Fat 7,6g 38%

Cholesterol 30,81mg 10%

Sodium 62,57mg 3%

Potassium 93,84mg 3%

Total Carbohydrates 32,47g 11%

Fiber 1,74g 7%

Sugar 7,14g

Protein 4,01g 8%

Oat - Flake Cookies with Raisins

Ingredients

1 1/2 cups flour for all uses

1 1/2 tsp baking powder

1 tsp cinnamon

1 pinch of salt

1 cup fresh butter unsalted

1 1/4 cups brown sugar

2 eggs, free-range

1 tsp vanilla powder

1 1/2 cups oat flakes

3/4 cup of raisins

Instructions

1. Soft at room temperature.
2. Preheat the oven to 350 °F/175 ° C.
3. Line a baking tray with parchment paper.
4. Stir the flour with baking powder, cinnamon, and salt.
5. In a separate bowl, beat butter and sugar for 1 minute.
6. Add the eggs and vanilla and continue to beat until all ingredients are combined well.
7. Add slowly a flour mixture; beat for further 2 -3 minutes.
8. Add the oat flakes and raisins and stir with a wooden spoon for one minute.
9. With a tablespoon scoop a butter and place on the baking pan, leaving some place between each cookie.
10. Bake for about 8 to 10 minutes.
11. Remove your cookies from the oven, and let them cool completely.
12. Store in a container and keep refrigerated for one week or place muffins in a freezer-safe bag, and keep in a freezer.

Servings: 12

Preparation Time: 30 minutes

Nutrition Facts

Serving size: 1/12 of a recipe (3.4 ounces)

Percent daily values based on the Reference Daily Intake (RDI) for a 2000 calorie diet.

Nutrition information calculated from recipe ingredients.

Amount Per Serving

Calories 379,98

Calories From Fat (39%) 149,27

% Daily Value

Total Fat 17g 26%

Saturated Fat 10,12g 51%

Cholesterol 71,67mg 24%

Sodium 108,9mg 5%

Potassium 184,8mg 5%

Total Carbohydrates 54,37g 18%

Fiber 1,94g 8%

Sugar 33,02g

Protein 4,51g 9%

Total Chocolate Cake

Ingredients

3/4 lb chocolate covertures cut into small chunks

1 1/2 cups Nutella chocolate-hazelnut spread

1 cup fresh butter

Instructions

1. Grease a square tray and set aside.
2. In a small saucepan, heat the covertures along with Nutella and butter over low heat.
3. Stir until the ingredients melt and combined well; stir frequently.
4. Pour the mixture on the prepared tray, and straighten the surface with the back of a spoon.
5. Refrigerate the cake overnight.

6. Remove the cake from refrigerator, cut into square pieces.
7. Store covered in the refrigerator for one week.
8. Store cake in a freezer-safe bag, and keep in a freezer for 3 months.

Servings: 8

Preparation Time: 15 minutes

Nutrition Facts

Serving size: 1/8 of a recipe (3.6 ounces)

Percent daily values based on the Reference Daily Intake (RDI) for a 2000 calorie diet.

Nutrition information calculated from recipe ingredients.

Amount Per Serving

Calories 449,67

Calories From Fat (78%) 348,99

% Daily Value

Total Fat 39,31g 60%

Saturated Fat 23,94g 120%

Cholesterol 63,56mg 21%

Sodium 7,37mg <1%

Potassium 247,93mg 7%

Total Carbohydrates 22,31g 7%

Fiber 3,4g 14%

Sugar 15,63g

Protein 2,84g 6%

Traditional Semolina Cake
with Syrup

Ingredients

1 1/2 cup coarse semolina

1 1/2 cup fine semolina

1 1/2 cup sugar

2 1/2 cups of yogurt

2 tsp of baking powder

1 tsp pure vanilla extract

<u>For the syrup:</u>

1 1/2 cup water

2 1/2 cup brown sugar (or stevia sweetener)

Instructions

1. Preheat oven to 360 F/180 C.
2. Grease a rectangular baking pan with a little oil and set aside.
3. Combine all ingredients in a mixing bowl; with electric mixer beat until compact mixture is achieved.
4. Pour the batter in a prepared baking pan.
5. Bake for 1 hour and 15 minutes.
6. Remove the cake from the oven and cut diagonally while it's still hot.
7. Cook water and sugar over medium heat for 5 - 6 minutes or until sugar is completely dissolved and you get a thick syrup.
8. Pour hot syrup over the cake.
9. Let cool on room temperature; cover with foil and keep refrigerated.
10. Store cake in a freezer-safe container, and keep in a freezer.

Servings: 14

Preparation Time: 1 hour and 30 minutes

Nutrition Facts

Serving size: 1/14 of a recipe (5.9 ounces)

Percent daily values based on the Reference Daily Intake (RDI) for a 2000 calorie diet.

Nutrition information calculated from recipe ingredients.

Amount Per Serving

Calories 389,82

Calories From Fat (2%) 9,08

% Daily Value

Total Fat 1,05g 2%

Saturated Fat 0,49g 2%

Cholesterol 2,63mg <1%

Sodium 112,64mg 5%

Potassium 222,44mg 6%

Total Carbohydrates 89,32g 30%

Fiber 1,4g 6%

Sugar 62,62g

Protein 6,88g 14%

VEGETARIAN

◆ ◆ ◆

Braised Cauliflower with Grated Tomato (Crock Pot)

Ingredients

2 lbs cauliflower flowerets

1/2 cup garlic-infused olive oil

1 large onion finely chopped

2 carrots, grated

1 cup of grated tomatoes

Salt and ground red pepper to taste

1/2 cup water

Instructions

1. Rinse the cauliflower, clean them and divide into floweret.
2. Brush the bottom of your Crock Pot with olive oil; add the cauliflower floweret.
3. Add the onion, grated carrots and tomatoes.
4. Season with the salt and ground red pepper; stir well.
5. Pour half cup water and stir again.
6. Cover and cook for on LOW setting for 3 to 4 hours or until tender.
7. Open and taste; adjust the salt and red pepper if needed.
8. Let cool on room temperature and then store in a fridge for 3 to 4 days.
9. Or, you can freeze your meal in airtight- freezer-safe bags or container.

Servings: 6

Preparation Time: 4 hours and 10 minutes

Nutrition Facts

Serving size: 1/6 of a recipe (11 ounces)

Percent daily values based on the Reference Daily Intake (RDI) for a 2000 calorie diet.

Nutrition information calculated from recipe ingredients.

Amount Per Serving

Calories 69,85

Calories From Fat (7%) 5,09

% Daily Value

Total Fat 0,61g < 1%

Saturated Fat 0,13g < 1%

Cholesterol 0mg 0%

Sodium 173,92mg 7%

Potassium 710,58mg 20%

Total Carbohydrates 15,02g 5%

Fiber 4,88g 20%

Sugar 6,83g

Protein 3,97g 8%

Braised Celeriac with Dill

Ingredients

2 medium celeriac cut in pieces

1 onion, finely chopped

2 carrots, scrubbed and sliced

1 Tbsp flour (all purpose or white whole wheat)

2 cups hot water

Juice from 2 lemons freshly squeezed

1 cup potato cut in cubes

2 tsp dill, finely chopped

1/2 cup of olive oil

Salt and freshly ground pepper

Instructions

1. Clean and cut the celeriac; pour the celeriac with the lemon juice immediately; set aside.
2. Heat the olive oil in a pot over moderate-high heat, on 400-450 degrees F.
3. Sauté the onion and carrots; add a pinch of salt and cook for about 5 - 6 minutes stirring occasionally.
4. Sprinkle with the flour and continue the sauté until golden brown.
5. Pour the hot water, lemon juice, potato, dill, salt, and pepper.
6. Stir well and cover the lid.
7. Cook for about 20 to 25 minutes over medium heat on 350 degrees F.
8. Remove from heat and let it cool on room temperature.
9. Refrigerate for two hours.
10. Transfer your meal in a freezer-safe container with cover, and store in a freezer.

Servings: 6

Preparation Time: 45 minutes

Total Time: 45 minutes

Nutrition Facts

Serving size: 1/6 of a recipe (9.6 ounces)

Percent daily values based on the Reference Daily Intake (RDI) for a 2000 calorie diet.

Nutrition information calculated from recipe ingredients.

Amount Per Serving

Calories 244,69

Calories From Fat (66%) 162,58

% Daily Value

Total Fat 18,41g 28%

Saturated Fat 2,58g 13%

Cholesterol 0mg 0%

Sodium 108,14mg 5%

Potassium 518,66mg 15%

Total Carbohydrates 19,37g 6%

Fiber 3,39g 14%

Sugar 3,97g

Protein 2,58g 5%

Dalmatian Braised Swiss Chard Dish

Ingredients

½ cup olive oil

4 cloves garlic, sliced thin

1 lb cauliflower floret

Kosher salt and freshly ground black pepper, to taste

1 cup water

1 large potato, peeled and diced

1 lb Swiss chard, tough stems removed, tender stems and leaves torn into 2" pieces

Lemon juice, freshly squeezed for serving

Instructions

1. Heat the oil in a pot over medium-high (400-450 degrees F) heat.
2. Cook the garlic with salt until soft, stir about 2 - 3 minutes.
3. Add chopped cauliflower, potato and pour water; cook over medium-low heat, stirring occasionally, for 10 minutes.
4. Add the Swiss chard; cook until wilted, about 5 minutes.
5. Taste and adjust salt and pepper if needed; stir.
6. Remove from the heat and let cool on room temperature.
7. Store in a refrigerator for 3 to 4 days or store in a freezer-safe container, and keep in a freezer.

Servings: 4

Preparation Time: 35 minutes

Cooking Time: 30 minutes

Nutrition Facts

Serving size: 1/4 of a recipe (13.4 ounces)

Percent daily values based on the Reference Daily Intake (RDI) for a 2000 calorie diet.

Nutrition information calculated from recipe ingredients.

Amount per Serving

Calories 254,31

Calories From Fat (65%) 164,43

% Daily Value

Total Fat 18,68g 29%

Saturated Fat 2,62g 13%

Cholesterol 0mg 0%

Sodium 281,78mg 12%

Potassium 1014,46mg 29%

Total Carbohydrates 21,79g 7%

Fiber 6,43g 26%

Sugar 3,8g

Protein 5,66g 11%

Green Bean Power Soup
(Slow Cooker)

Ingredients

1/2 lb fresh green beans

1 onion cut in rings

2 cloves garlic, crushed

2 cups grated fresh tomato

2 cups water

2 cups vegetable broth

1 tsp fresh thyme, finely chopped

1 tsp fresh chives finely chopped

Salt and ground pepper to taste

Instructions

1. Place all ingredients in your Slow Cooker.
2. Cover and cook on LOW 4 - 5 hours.
3. Taste and adjust salt and pepper if needed.
4. Keep refrigerated for 3 days or freeze in a freezer-safe container.
5. Reheat in a microwave and enjoy!

Servings: 6

Preparation Time: 5 hours

Nutrition Facts

Serving size: 1/6 of a recipe (9.8 ounces)

Percent daily values based on the Reference Daily Intake (RDI) for a 2000 calorie diet.

Nutrition information calculated from recipe ingredients.

Amount per Serving

Calories 55,85

Calories From Fat (14%) 8,06

% Daily Value

Total Fat 1,91g 3%

Saturated Fat 0,72g 4%

Cholesterol 0mg 0%

Sodium 57,57mg 2%

Potassium 434,91mg 12%

Total Carbohydrates 7,36g 2%

Fiber 2,2g 9%

Sugar 3,69g

Protein 12,2g 24%

Mediterranean Green Beans with Potato

Ingredients

1 1/2 lbs of green beans, cleaned

2 potatoes cut in cubes

1 carrot cut in slices

1 onion finely chopped

1/2 lb grated tomato

1 cup of chopped parsley

1 1/2 cup of hot water

1 tsp sugar

1/4 cup olive oil

Salt and ground black pepper

Instructions

1. Rinse your green beans and then clean them by cutting the two edges.
2. Heat the oil in a deep pot over medium-high heat.
3. Sauté the onion, potatoes, and carrot for 5 to 6 minutes stirring occasionally.
4. Sprinkle with salt, pepper, and little sugar.
5. Add the green beans and stir to combine all ingredients for 6 to 8 minutes.
6. Add grated tomatoes, pour warm water and stir.
7. Cook uncovered over low heat for about 20 minutes.
8. At this point, add some more salt and pepper and parsley; stir.
9. Cook for further 10 to 15 minutes.
10. Leave to cool at room temperature and combine the flavors.
11. Store in refrigerator for 3 to 5 days or freeze in airtight containers with cover.

Servings: 6

Preparation Time: 55 minutes

Nutrition Facts

Serving size: 1/6 of a recipe (10.4 ounces)

Percent daily values based on the Reference Daily Intake (RDI) for a 2000 calorie diet.

Nutrition information calculated from recipe ingredients.

Amount Per Serving

Calories 171,74

Calories From Fat (48%) 81,84

% Daily Value

Total Fat 9,27g 14%

Saturated Fat 1,31g 7%

Cholesterol 0mg 0%

Sodium 21,35mg < 1%

Potassium 498,13mg 14%

Total Carbohydrates 20,98g 7%

Fiber 4,57g 18%

Sugar 4,03g

Protein 3,15g 6%

Edward Cruz

Vegetable and Almond Para-
dise Patties

Ingredients

1/2 cup green olives rinsed and drained

2 green onions (scallions) finely chopped

2 onions freshly chopped

1/2 cup parsley finely chopped

1/2 tsp dill finely chopped

3 cups almond flour or finely ground almonds

1 cup sparkling water (or more if needed)

1 Tbsp baking soda

Salt and freshly ground black pepper

1 cup olive oil for frying

Instructions

1. Combine olives, green onion, onion, parsley, dill in a bowl; stir well.
2. Add the almond flour (or ground almonds) together with sparkling water; stir or knead to achieve a thick batter.
3. Season with the salt the pepper, add herbs and stir to combine well.
4. Heat the oil in a large frying skillet over high heat.
5. Take a spoonful of the mixture every time and fry patties until golden brown from both sides.
6. Transfer patties on a kitchen towel to drain.
7. Let sit at room temperature not more than one hour.
8. Store in a container, cover and keep in refrigerator up to 4 days.

Servings: 6

Preparation Time: 15 minutes

Nutrition Facts

Serving size: 1/6 of a recipe (7.7 ounces)

Percent daily values based on the Reference Daily Intake (RDI)

Edward Cruz

for a 2000 calorie diet.

Nutrition information calculated from recipe ingredients.

Amount Per Serving

Calories 198,17

Calories From Fat (88%) 174,82

% Daily Value

Total Fat 19,84g 31%

Saturated Fat 2,74g 14%

Cholesterol 0mg 0%

Sodium 831,05mg 35%

Potassium 103,36mg 3%

Total Carbohydrates 5,53g 2%

Fiber 1,53g 6%

Sugar 1,89g

Protein 0,81g 2%

PIES/PASTRIES

◆ ◆ ◆

Cheesy Mushrooms - Bacon Pie

Ingredients

2 Tbsp garlic-infused olive oil

1 large onion chopped

1 1/2 cans of mushrooms

1/4 cup grated Cheddar cheese

1/4 cup grated Gruyere cheese

1/4 cup grated Parmesan cheese

1 cup of cream

2 sheets of puff pastry

Instructions

1. Preheat the oven to 325F/160C.
2. Heat the oil in a deep frying pan and sauté the onion, mushrooms, and bacon for 3 - 4 minutes.
3. Add Cheddar, Gruyere and Parmesan cheese; stir over low heat until cheese is completely melted.
4. Lay one puff pastry on a greased baking sheet, pour the mushroom/cheese mixture, spread it evenly and add the second puff pastry on top.
5. Cut the top sheet only in pieces and pour over the cream.
6. Place in the oven and bake for 25 - 30 minutes.
7. Remove from the oven and let it cool completely.
8. Slice and store in a container and keep refrigerated up to 5 days.
9. Or, you can freeze your pie in freezer safe bags for up to 2 months.

Servings: 8

Preparation Time: 50 minutes

Nutrition Facts

Serving size: 1/8 of a recipe (4.6 ounces)

Percent daily values based on the Reference Daily Intake (RDI) for a 2000 calorie diet.

Nutrition information calculated from recipe ingredients.

Amount Per Serving

Calories 551,98

Calories From Fat (70%) 384,87

% Daily Value

Total Fat 43,22g 66%

Saturated Fat 15,74g 79%

Cholesterol 50,93mg 17%

Sodium 260,86mg 11%

Potassium 106,86mg 3%

Total Carbohydrates 32,92g 11%

Fiber 1,3g 5%

Sugar 1,31g

Protein 8,89g 18%

Pumpkin Pie with Feta

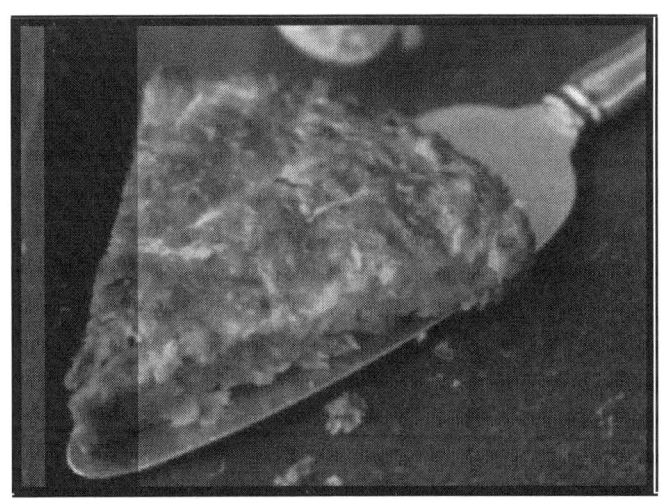

Ingredients

2 lbs pumpkin puree, canned

5 eggs from free-range chicken

1 1/2 cups of Feta, crumbled

1 cup of breadcrumbs

2 Tbsp dill finely chopped

2 Tbsp mint chopped

5 fresh onions with their leaves finely chopped

1/4 fl oz olive oil

Salt and ground pepper to taste

1/4 cup of olive oil

Instructions

1. Preheat oven to 170C/340F.
2. Lightly brush a small baking sheet and sprinkle it with the half of bread crumbles.
3. Add the pumpkin puree, eggs, cheese, and rest of bread crumble the dill, and the mint, as well as the fresh onions.
4. Grind a lot of pepper and salt, after trying the mixture.
5. Spread the mixture into the baking pan.
6. Bake for 40-45 minutes, until the surface, is slightly browned.
7. Remove from the oven and let it cool.
8. Store in the refrigerator for 5 days.
9. Store in freezer-safe container or bag, and keep in a freezer.

Servings: 10

Preparation Time: 1 hour and 10 minutes

Nutrition Facts

Serving size: 1/10 of a recipe (5.8 ounces)

Percent daily values based on the Reference Daily Intake (RDI) for a 2000 calorie diet.

Nutrition information calculated from recipe ingredients.

Amount Per Serving

Calories 211,45

Calories From Fat (59%) 125,38

% Daily Value

Total Fat 14,17g 22%

Saturated Fat 5,2g 26%

Cholesterol 113,03mg 38%

Sodium 433,81mg 18%

Potassium 350,36mg 10%

Total Carbohydrates 12,66g 4%

Fiber 1,71g 7%

Sugar 4,13g

Protein 9,16g 18%

Perfect Crustless Sausage, Mushrooms and Spinach Quiche

Ingredients

1/4 cup olive oil

1 spring onion, finely diced

3/4 cup mushrooms, sliced

8 oz Italian sausages sliced

3 egg whites

6 free-range large eggs

1/2 cup milk

1/2 cup Cheddar cheese

1 cup spinach

Salt and ground pepper to taste

Instructions

1. Preheat oven to 400 degrees F/200 C.
2. Heat the oil in a large frying skillet and sauté spring onion and mushrooms for 2 - 3 minutes or until soft.
3. Remove skillet from heat and set aside.
4. In the same skillet, add sausages and cook about 5 minutes over.
5. Add the mushrooms and onions back to the pan.
6. In a large bowl, whisk together eggs, milk, salt, and pepper.
7. Pour the egg mixture over the sausage mixture in the pan over medium-low.
8. Stir in cheese and fresh spinach leaves.
9. Bake for 40-50 minutes.
10. Let it cold and cut into pieces.
11. Store wrapped quiche slices in your freezer for two months.

Servings: 6

Preparation Time: 1 hour and 15 minutes

Nutrition Facts

Serving size: 1/6 of a recipe (6.1 ounces)

Percent daily values based on the Reference Daily Intake (RDI) for a 2000 calorie diet.

Nutrition information calculated from recipe ingredients.

Amount per Serving

Calories 303,08

Calories From Fat (73%) 219,73

% Daily Value

Total Fat 24,75g 38%

Saturated Fat 7,07g 35%

Cholesterol 227,71mg 76%

Sodium 523,81mg 22%

Potassium 207,27mg 6%

Total Carbohydrates 3,01g 1%

Fiber 0,3g 1%

Sugar 1,7g

Protein 17,38g 35%

Potato Pie with Soft Goat Cheese

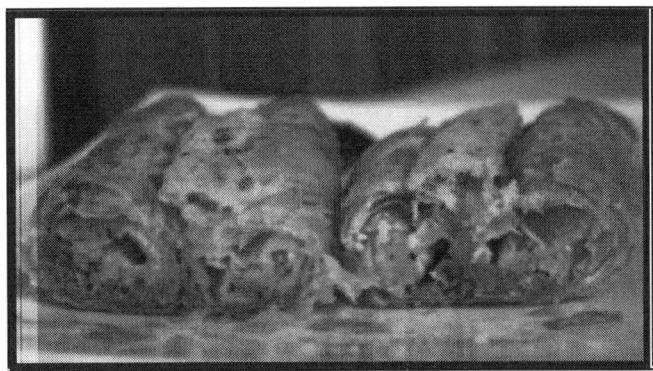

Ingredients

1 lb of flour

2 cups of olive oil

1 Tbsp vinegar

Lukewarm water (as needed)

2 large onions cut in thin washers

2 lbs of potatoes in cubes

2 eggs

2 cups of soft goat cheese

2 Tbsp fresh basil leaves finely chopped

Salt and ground black pepper

1 cup of milk

Instructions

1. Preheat oven to 360 F / 180C.
2. Put the flour in a bowl, open a hole in the center and pour the oil and vinegar.
3. Pour lukewarm water and knead the dough.
4. In a non-stick pan, heat a splash of olive oil and sauté the onions until soft.
5. Add the potatoes, stir and simmer for 15 minutes.
6. After boiling, remove from the heat and allow them to cool.
7. Beat the eggs in a bowl and add the goat cheese, basil, and the salt and pepper
8. Add the potatoes, pressing with a fork to get a uniform texture.
9. Take the dough and make 4 to 4 thick sheets.
10. Cut every sheet in half lengthwise and spread a generously the potato filling along the sheet and wrap it in a roll.
11. Place the roll it in an oiled pan.
12. Do the same with all the sheets and place in a baking pan.
13. In a bowl, whisk some oil and milk and pour over your pie.
14. Bake for 50 minutes.
15. Let the pie cool completely and slice.
16. Place in a container and keep refrigerated for 4 - 5 days.

Servings: 14

Preparation Time: 1 hour and 20 minutes

Nutrition Facts

Serving size: 1/14 of a recipe (6.5 ounces)

Percent daily values based on the Reference Daily Intake (RDI) for a 2000 calorie diet.

Nutrition information calculated from recipe ingredients.

Amount per Serving

Calories 414,98

Calories From Fat (50%) 209,02

% Daily Value

Total Fat 23,69g 36%

Saturated Fat 7,38g 37%

Cholesterol 46,02mg 15%

Sodium 142,22mg 6%

Potassium 421,52mg 12%

Total Carbohydrates 39,51g 13%

Fiber 2,84g 11%

Sugar 2,83g

Protein 11,4g 23%

Traditional Cretan Tomato Pie

Ingredients

2 cups all-purpose flour

1/2 tsp dried yeast

1/2 tsp of salt

1 tsp of Italian herbs

1 Tbsp of honey

1 Tbsp of fresh butter

1/2 cup lukewarm water

1/4 cup of olive oil

4 cloves of garlic finely chopped

2 lbs of tomatoes, peeled, without seeds

1 Tbsp of tomato paste

Salt and freshly ground pepper

1 tsp oregano

1 tsp of thyme

1/2 cup of feta cheese grated

1/2 cup of grated Gouda cheese

Instructions

1. In a bowl, stir the flour with yeast, salt, and herbs.
2. Create a hole in the center and pour the honey and butter.
3. Pour water and stir all ingredients; knead for 10-12 minutes by hand or 8 - 10 minutes with the mixer.
4. Cover with a plastic film and leave it in a warm, humid place for 1 hour to double in volume.
5. At the same time, heat the oil in a saucepan, and sauté garlic with a pinch of salt.
6. Pour the tomato sauce, tomato paste, oregano, thyme, and the salt and pepper; simmer for 30 minutes over low heat.
7. Preheat oven to 400 F/200 C.
8. Open the dough in a sheet and place in a pizza pan.
9. Apply the tomato mixture over the dough, and sprinkle the surface with oregano and thyme.
10. Sprinkle with grated Gouda and Feta cheese.
11. Bake in the oven for 25 minutes or until the pie is golden brown.
12. Remove from the oven and let cool on room temperature.
13. Slice and store in a container with the lid.

14. Keep refrigerated up to one week.

Servings: 10

Preparation Time: 1 hour and 15 minutes

Inactive Time: 1 hour

Nutrition Facts

Serving size: 1/10 of a recipe (5.8 ounces)

Percent daily values based on the Reference Daily Intake (RDI) for a 2000 calorie diet.

Nutrition information calculated from recipe ingredients.

Amount per Serving

Calories 231,89

Calories From Fat (43%) 100,05

% Daily Value

Total Fat 11,37g 17%

Saturated Fat 4,43g 22%

Cholesterol 21,13mg 7%

Sodium 301,02mg 13%

Potassium 286,49mg 8%

Total Carbohydrates 25,92g 9%

Fiber 2,05g 8%

Sugar 4,93g

Protein 7,22g 14%

Wild Greens Pie with Feta and Yoghurt

Ingredients

3 spring onions finely chopped

2 Tbsp olive oil

2 Tbsp butter

1 leek, chopped

1 clove garlic

2 spring onions

2 lbs of various wild greens (amaranth, dandelion green-

s...etc.)

Salt and pepper to taste

1 cup yogurt

2 medium eggs

1 lb Feta cheese

1 bunch of fresh dill

1 bunch of fresh parsley

1 bunch of fresh mint

Zest from 2 lemons

1/2 cup of olive oil

Pie Crusts

Instructions

1. Preheat the oven to 350 ° F/ 170 C.
2. Place a non-stick pan on high heat.
3. Add the olive oil and the butter.
4. Sauté the onion, leek, and garlic for about 5 minutes.
5. Add the white parts of the fresh onions and keep the green part aside.
6. Add the greens, the white part of the fresh onions, salt, pepper and stir for 3-4 minutes.
7. Transfer the mixture to a bowl, and let it cool down.
8. Combine the onion mixture with yogurt, eggs, and white cheese.
9. Open the pie crust sheets.
10. Sprinkle with olive oil every sheet.
11. Place 2 pie sheets together and fill with the onion/wild

greens/yogurt mixture.

12. Sprinkle over with chopped free dill, mint and parsley.
13. In the end, sprinkle with lemon zest.
14. Cover with two pie sheets; grease the surface with the olive oil.
15. Turn the edges in and draw the pot with a knife.
16. Place in oven and bake for 70 minutes.
17. Remove from the oven and let cool at room temperature.
18. Cut in slices and store in containers; cover with the lid. Keep refrigerated for one week.
19. Or, store a pie in freezer-safe container or bag, and keep in a freezer.

Servings: 8

Preparation Time: 1 hour and 40 minutes

Nutrition Facts

Serving size: 1/8 of a recipe (11 ounces)

Percent daily values based on the Reference Daily Intake (RDI) for a 2000 calorie diet.

Nutrition information calculated from recipe ingredients.

Amount per Serving

Calories 496,49

Calories From Fat (69%) 340,16

% Daily Value

Total Fat 38,47g 59%

Saturated Fat 14,92g 75%

Cholesterol 106,43mg 35%

Sodium 847,41mg 35%

Potassium 952,99mg 27%

Total Carbohydrates 24,77g 8%

Fiber 1,86g 7%

Sugar 7,73g

Protein 15,96g 32%

BONUS BOOK

http://bit.ly/2Z1N6oj

About the Author

Edward Cruz is the #1 Amazon best-selling author of *How to lose belly fat: meal plans for ultimate weight loss for men and women in 8 weeks* among others. He lives in Chacago, Illinois with his family.

"I am not going to mislead you and promise that you will lose weight in a week - like many "teachers" do, while they cannot bring their own bodies in shape!

I will simply show you a working method that has helped me and many of my clients to keep our bodies toned and shaped at all times and achieve this in a fairly short time.

But the most important thing is that this technique will help you to lose weight at last and change your life forever!"

One Last Thing...

If you enjoyed this book or found it useful I'd be very grateful if you'd post a short review on Amazon. Your support really does make a difference and I read all the reviews personally so I can get your feedback and make this book even better.

If you'd like to leave a review then all you need to do is click the review link on this book's page on Amazon here:

I strongly believe that the advice in here can help people with their weight loss goals and you can help too by spreading the word.

If you think this book could be better in any way you can let me know what needs to be improved by sending an email to **perfectecruz@gmail.com**.

I can then update this and future books and provide the best information so that you and others can get even more value from this book.

Thanks again for your support!

Made in the USA
Columbia, SC
22 August 2019